WAR

AND

WEAPON

An Illustrated Legacy of the Ahom Military

SAURADEEP NATH

INDIA • SINGAPORE • MALAYSIA

ISBN
Hardcase 979-8-89724-791-2
Paperback 979-8-89673-483-3

Dedicated to

Prof. Sajal Nag

Contents

Foreword

India had two important gateways through which myriad migratory groups entered the land and settled here. One was the North Western Frontier Gate, and the other was the North Eastern Frontier Gate. Right from the Aryans to the Mughals had entered India through the North Western Gateway, whereas hordes of South East Asian Mongoloid tribes entered India and settled in its northeastern and eastern India. One of them was the Tai-Ahoms of Assam. Ahoms were one of the Shan tribes of South East Asia who migrated to the Brahmaputra valley of Assam to settle and establish a kingdom that lasted for about six hundred years. Although it was not an invasion but migration yet whatever opposition they encountered on the way had to be dealt with through warfare. Even after entering the Valley, they encountered a number of small chieftaindoms and autochthones who were subjugated to establish their kingdom. The nature of adversaries ranged from opposition on the migratory route to the resistance offered by the indigenous settled tribes. Major wars were the Ahom-Chutiya war in 1523 CE, the Ahom-Dimasa war, which continued till the 19th century CE; the Ahom-Mughal war in the 17th century; and finally, the Burmese invasion of Assam. In this entire process, it was their weaponry that helped them win the wars and opposition that they faced. Some of these weapons were brought from the place of their origin, and some were designed in the course of their settlement with the help of local artisans, available minerals, and the nature of warfare. The present work encompasses the documentation and analysis of Ahom weapons, which were studied from the specimens preserved and displayed in museums across Assam. The author categorises the weapons into melee weapons, ranged weapons, and defensive weapons; and then, based on the availability of Ahom melee weapons, they were again sub-divided into pointed weapons, which include spears, and edged weapons, which include swords. Similarly, ranged weapons were divided based on propulsion technique, and as such, based on explosive propulsion, Ahom firearms were studied. However, due to the absence of tangible specimens, the study could only manage to elicit the names of Ahom bow and arrow, which were based on elastic propulsion. Likewise, defensive weapons, mostly shields, were under observation in the study. The study also informs us regarding the organization of Ahom armed forces. the Ahom military organization, their armed engagement against varied adversaries, and their way of mining, smelting, and forging technology, and the Ahom sources of iron ore and pig-iron. The book is a minefield of information on a subject which is rarely dealt with. He uses deft analysis to develop deep insight about the military practices of Ahom Assam. I strongly recommend the book to anyone who is reading history of medieval Assam.

Sajal Nag
Distinguished Professor
Assam Royal Global University
Guwahati

Preface

Somewhere deep down, a scholar needs to find the reason behind preparing a manuscript. After reading a couple of "prefaces," I have understood that a preface elicits a scholar's perspective on drafting a manuscript. Hence, in light of this apprehension, I am extending my views toward formulating and presenting the book before the readers, who can further discuss and criticize the work.

It won't be wrong to say that the book is an extension of my Ph.D. work. Since my Ph.D. study concentrated on only one aspect of Ahom weaponry, i.e., edged weapons, it neglected other types of weaponry, such as ranged and defensive weapons. Thus, speaking boldly to bridge the limitations of my Ph.D. work, this monograph is compiled, including weapons that were not previously studied or documented. In this process, Ahom weapons, preserved and displayed in museums across Assam, are analyzed and described.

Yet, I would say that nuances do exist in the current work, and I hope to be dealt with by future researchers in the field. I must say that the aspect and prospect of studies in weapons are novel, as far as the Northeastern Region of India is concerned. Articles and monographs are limited, and so is the methodology involved with its study. Thus, the monograph attempts to limit ignorance, with high hopes to imbibe curiosity among readers and researchers alike to take up the study, discover new avenues, and fill the knowledge gap.

Besides that, the monograph is also an outcome of an ardent desire to elicit the tangible heritage of the Ahom and Assam before the community in a scientific way. I think we should not feel shy to acknowledge that we live in a world of social media where every other aspect of life is displayed on digital screens, including weapons. Yet what social media limits we academicians tend to provide, i.e., a scientific approach and an unbiased narrative of cultural heritage. The monograph offers an account of Ahom weapons that goes beyond what one usually finds on social media. With such prospects in mind, I urge the readers to delve into the book, for it is "you" for whom it is written. Please feel free to extend your valuable suggestions.

Acknowledgment

What acknowledgment means to me can be best expressed by Sir Isaac Newton's quote, which is found in a letter addressed to fellow scientist Robert Hooke, dated 5 February 1675. The quote goes like this, "If I have seen further, it is by standing on the shoulders of giants." Thus, what I am now and what my work represents is the consequence of the contribution of many before me and those contemporaries around me from academic and non-academic backgrounds.

No work on the Ahom can be done without referring to the edited and translated *Buranji* of Dr. S.K. Bhuyan. His invaluable contribution, and the works of fellow scholars, such as R.M. Nath's (1948) *The Background of the Assamese Culture*, H. Borboruah's (1981) *Ahomar Din*, S.L. Baruah's (1985) *A Comprehensive History of Assam*, H.K. Barpujari's (1992) *The Comprehensive History of Assam*, D. Baishya (2009) *Traditional Science and Material Culture of Early Assam*, K. Gogoi (2017) *Ahom Warfare Evolution, Nature, and Strategy*, etc. have immensely enriched my work, and if not for them my work would not have seen daylight.

Teachers play a pivotal role in shaping and nurturing pupils—my teachers from school and college, like Mr. Manoj Kr. Nath, Mr. Amit Singha, Mr. Krishna Mohan Singh, Dr. Dhrubojyoti Dey, and Mr. Rajang Narzary, and professors from Assam University, like Prof. Alok Tripathi, Prof. Sajal Nag, Prof. Sudeshna Purkayastha, and Prof. Projit Palit, did the same. They groomed me and honed my skills, leaving a deep impression that I will cherish forever.

For data collection, I had to visit museums, and everywhere I went, I was welcomed with warm hospitality from officers, staff, and people in general. When I think of such personnel, the name of Jorhat's District Museum Officer, Mrs. Abantika Parashar, comes first. She has been a beacon in my journey as a scholar so far. Mrs. Shenamoni Chetia of Ahom-Tai Museum, Sivasagar, is another person who taught me many things regarding artifacts, and so did Mr. Vidya Phukan. Abhilash Rajkhowa of District Museum in Tezpur, Antareen Talukdar of Directorate of Museum in Guwahati, Gautam Ojha of District Museum in Mangaldoi, Jaylal Basfor of Srimanta Sankardeva Kalakshetra, Mrs. Snigdha Hasnu Curator of Assam State Museum in Guwahati, and Mr. Y.S. Wunglengton, former Director of Museum, Assam are some few officers whose name I can recollect and mention.

Then there are my friends whose doors were always open for me. They have been a constant source of encouragement in the journey. Dr. Nayan Jyoti Pathak is one such person whose *being* in life is a blessing. Dr. Shring Dao Langthasa is another whose input made me a better researcher. Sangeeta Shyam Gohain's name should also be mentioned, for she showed great interest in my craft.

There is also my family, who always stood by me like a mountain, no matter the circumstance. Special thanks to my mother, Ava Debi; nothing would have been possible without her. She entirely funded my research for the book while believing in me when no one else did. Her faith and blessings motivate and move me forward. My aunt Purnima Nath, who made sure I ate food and took care of my health; my uncle Chuni Lal Nath, who took care of other affairs in my absence; and at last, my dearest younger brother Ratnadeep Nath, whose wisdom enriches my soul, put me at solace. He is the brightest of all and for whom is the beginning and end. I also bow to my late father, Prabir Ch. Nath, whose blessings always bestow upon me.

Lastly, I would like to thank my publisher, Notion Press, and its team for publishing the monograph and the readers on whose hands the book lies. It is for you that the book has been compiled, and now you are the custodian of this wealth. My forever gratitude remains with you.

Chapter 01

Introduction

The Ahom belong to the Tai ethnic group. The term 'Tai' refers to a vast ethnic group with different branches inhabiting an area extending from Assam in the Republic of India to the Guangxi Zhuang Autonomous Region in China (officially the People's Republic of China) and Thailand (officially the Kingdom of Thailand). The Tai ethnicity and its various subgroups are known by various regional names. For example, in Myanmar (officially the Republic of the Union of Myanmar), the Tai are referred to as 'Shan,' 'Thai' in Thailand, 'Lao' in Laos (officially the Lao People's Democratic Republic), and 'Zhuang' in China. Similarly, the Tai-Mao branch, known as Shan in Myanmar, which arrived in the *Nam-Ti-Lao*[1] (Brahmaputra) Valley in the 13th century CE, is known by its indigenous name, 'Ahom.'

Although contributions associated with Ahom history, culture, and archaeology are manifold, studies on their weapons are few. Consider the go-to-book of history enthusiasts for delving into Assam's medieval history, Gait's (1905) *A History of Assam*. In the book, Gait describes the political history of the Ahom dynasty while making scanty references to Ahom weapons, such as swords, spears, and firearms. Likewise, although Baruah's (1985) work *A Comprehensive History of Assam* delves a bit deeper into the subject of weapons as she made certain clarifications regarding the earliest usage of firearms, there were limitations. Later, Barpujari's (1994) edited volume, *The Comprehensive History of Assam*, made justice to Ahom weapons as it dedicated a separate segment where a wide range of weapons were classified into offensive and defensive types. Continuation of works in this direction resulted in Gogoi's (2006) article, *War Weapons in Medieval Assam*, and Gogoi's (2017) unpublished thesis, *Ahom Warfare: Evolution, Nature, and Strategy*. Both these works dealt with Ahom weapons in their respective ways. Yet, it more or less followed the same tradition of citing only the name from the *Buranji*[2] (Ahom chronicle).

Of course, there is no denying that prior studies did contribute. Yet, the name alone does not satisfy our curiosity, nor does it answer the questions, such as what were the various types of Ahom weapons? Can the Ahom weapon be classified in the conventional manner of offensive and defensive types, or should a new approach be developed? Do we have tangible Ahom weapons in museums across Assam? If so, how can these be documented, i.e., what methodology should be followed? Will the tangible sources and subsequent documentation resolve the knowledge gap, if not entirely, at least partially? Who were the people engaged in forging weapons? From where were the Ahom procuring pig iron for forging? Did they have an indigenous source, or were they procuring it elsewhere? If from other places, then what was the nature of procurement, was it through trade or by tribute?

Hence, to delve into these queries, the present study is undertaken. The study's objectives are as follows–identify the Ahom weapons preserved and displayed in Assam's museums; classify the Ahom weapons in a novel way, along with mentioning the reason behind such classification; develop a novel methodology for documenting weapons; enumerate the Ahom sources of iron ore; and discuss in length the Ahom mining, smelting, and forging process.

Scope of the Study

As the title suggests, the study's scope encompasses the documentation and analysis of Ahom weapons preserved and displayed in museums across Assam. In this process, the weapons were first grouped into melee weapons, ranged weapons, and defensive weapons; and then, based on the availability of Ahom melee weapons in museums, they were again divided into pointed weapons (e.g., spears) and edged weapons, (e.g., swords). Similarly, ranged weapons were divided based on propulsion technique, and as such, based on explosive propulsion, Ahom firearms were studied. However, due to the absence of tangible specimens, the work could only manage to elicit the Ahom bow and arrow names, which were based on elastic propulsion. Likewise, defensive weapons, mostly shields, were studied.

Nevertheless, the scope is not only limited to documenting weapons but also includes introducing a novel methodology for documenting weapons of various types. This is done by providing three different pro forma sheets, each for a different type of weapon. The sheets are standardized and designed with the hopes that scholars will use them for studying weapons in the future. Besides, the study also delved into the use of weapons in combat. As such, the Ahom military engagement from the establishment of the Ahom kingdom in the 13th century CE till the 19th century CE is furnished chronologically.

Moreover, there is also an inquiry regarding the organization of Ahom armed forces. This aspect is also subjected to the study. Lastly, the Ahom's sources of iron ore are re-evaluated through scrutiny of primary and secondary literary sources. As it turns out, earlier scholars missed the tribute aspect of the pig iron collection by the Ahom. Thus, a corroborative approach combines the tangible observation with the account left in the literature to create a comprehensive account of the Ahom weapon.

Methodology

With a few exceptions, such as Nath (2023), Nath (2024), and Tripathi and Nath (2024), studies on Ahom weapons through material remains are rare until the current work. Though scholars based on the Ahom chronicles elicited the names of Ahom weapons, their corroboration with those preserved at museums across Assam has never been attempted. Of course, museum catalogs enumerate the dimensions and weights of each weapon displayed at the respective museum. Yet proper measurements highlighting every aspect of these are unavailable without primary observation and documentation. Thus, the author developed a method for recording the details of Ahom weapons preserved and displayed at multiple institutions. Three separate pro forma sheets--one for recording edged weapons (appendix 1), another for firearms (appendix 2), and a third for shields (appendix 3) were prepared. These sheets were designed to ensure no data or information is missed.

For instance, the sheet on edged weapon records information of provenance, date, accession number, and damage or decoration (on either blade or hilt) of a particular sword, spear, or chopper, along with its full length, weight, and point of balance (from the tip). Besides, on the same sheet, data on the blade, such as length, width, thickness, cross-section, ricasso length, fuller length, and blade point, is noted. Similarly, hilt data is recorded on the sheet's separate section, including hilt length, cross-section, langet length, ferrule length, crossguard length, and pommel shape and radius.

Likewise, the sheet on firearm records information on provenance, date, accession number, overall condition, and inscription in the firearm. Besides, full length, weight, barrel length, trunnion length and diameter, vent hole diameter, muzzle's external diameter, bore diameter, knob length, and circumference, breech's external diameter, vent to breech base length, trunnion to muzzle length, and trunnion to breech base length are also recorded in the same sheet. On the other hand, the pro forma sheet on the shield records information related to provenance, date, accession number, weight, shape, diameter, and decoration or damage (if any). The measurements are taken using precise hand tapes and a digital vernier caliper. The recording system is standardized, and therefore, the methodology employed can be applied to record other weapons in various institutions in the future.

Nevertheless, concerning the study's aim, the method constitutes documenting and analyzing the weapon and corroborating it with information provided in the chronicles. These chronicles, accessed at the Department of Historical and Antiquarian Studies (DHAS) in Guwahati, Assam, provide valuable information on the utility of weapons in warfare and socio-religious ceremonies. This additional information has enabled us to explore the significance of weapons beyond martial to ceremonial purposes and classify them in a novel way. Besides, residents who have adequate knowledge of the oral tradition of earlier generations and blacksmiths who practice the age-old technique of forging were also interviewed. The interviews were conducted in Assamese, i.e., *Oxomiya*, an Indo-European language, i.e., the lingua franca among many ethnic groups in Assam. Thus, the study delves into a broader context of weapons and their multifarious utility.

Organization of Chapter

The book is divided into seven chapters. The first chapter introduces the book, where a brief literature review of earlier and recent works on Ahom weapons is acknowledged, and the limitations and problems associated with these studies are mentioned. Besides, the chapter also includes the study's scope, which is not just limited to documentation and analysis of weapons but also provides a novel methodology of documentation, eliciting the Ahom military organization, their armed engagement against varied adversaries, and their way of mining, smelting, and forging technology. The study's objective demanded a methodology that could corroborate the information provided in literary sources with objective analysis of weapons preserved in museums across Assam. The methodology, as such, is also elaborated in the chapter along with a brief note on chapterisation.

The second chapter elaborates on Ahom's military engagement for nearly six hundred years against neighboring ethnic groups and kingdoms. In doing so, discussion has been made of the Ahom-Chutiya war and the later's subsequent defeat and annexation of their kingdom in 1523 CE; the Ahom-Dimasa war, which continued till 19th century CE; the Ahom-Mughal war in the 17th century CE, and so on. Besides the armed engagement, discussion on the Ahom military organization and its division into infantry, cavalry, elephantry, navy, and artillery is enumerated. Lastly, a brief note on various types of Ahom weapons is also elicited.

The third chapter discusses various types of Ahom melee weapons. The chapter begins with a definition and classification of melee weapons into two, i.e., pointed weapon and edged weapon, then a detailed description of Ahom pointed weapons preserved and displayed in museums of Assam, such as *Jathi* or flat spear (n=10), *Barsha* or leaf-shaped spear (n=4), and *Khapor* or multi-barbed spear (n=1) is furnished. Next, in terms of Ahom edged weapons description has been made of swords including *Hengdang* (n=2), *Torowal* (n=6), and *Da* or chopper, including *Nakoi-da* (n=8) and *Shikara-da* (n=1). Here, a discussion on the Ahom-Dimasa relation and Ahom-Miri relation is furnished to understand the acquisition of the above-mentioned choppers from the *Timisa* (Dimasa) kingdom and the Miri ethnic group, respectively.

The fourth chapter is on ranged weapons, where, along with the definition, its types--firearm and bow and arrow--are also described. Regarding the firearm, we have tried to clarify our understanding of its earliest usage by examining the colonial reports and chronicles. Following this, the chapter describes two types of Ahom firearm, i.e., *Bortop* or heavy artillery (n=23) and *Hilloi* or light artillery (n=10). Besides, the measurements of cannon balls (n=50) from various museums are also provided, along with a brief note on the varieties of bows and arrows used by the Ahom.

A short and separate chapter on Ahom's defensive weapon is also provided, followed by a sixth chapter, which discusses the Ahom sources of iron ore and pig iron. Besides delving into the mining, smelting, and forging process, the chapter also elicits the ethnic composition of smelters and blacksmiths who were organized into separate guilds. A discussion of the pig-iron trade between Ahom and Khasi is also included in the chapter, along with its acquisition as a tribute. The last concluding chapter provides a summary and key findings of the study.

Chapter 02

Ahom Military: War and Organisation

The Ahom kingdom flourished in the Brahmaputra Valley against many adversities till the English East India Company annexed it in the 19th century CE. Their triumph in the valley through the expansion of their kingdom and subsequent defense against invaders, such as the Turko-Afghan and the Mughal, requires a vivid description. The pages below are dedicated to Ahom's armed engagement in chronological order.

Ahom Military Engagement

The Ahom under Sukapha left their native land, *Mongmao*[3], in 1215 CE. According to the chronicles, he was accompanied by his family, including three wives, two sons, and one daughter. The strength of his followers included five *Mong* (province) chiefs, a contingent of nine thousand people, three hundred horses, and two elephants (Barua 1930, p. 44; Bhuyan 1932, p. 5; Bhuyan 1945, pp. 4-5; Bhuyan 1960, p. 2). During his journey, Sukapha first fought against the villagers of Mogaung, who resisted his advance. Then, after crossing the Khamjang River,[4] Sukapha halted near Nongyang Lake.[5] According to *Ahom Buranji* (Barua 1930), Sukapha ordered his chiefs to fight against the Naga of that area. Subsequently, the Naga villages of Kharukhu, Pungkang, Tithan, Binglao, Latema, Lanpang, and Taru submitted, whereas the villages of Luknam and Luka were destroyed by the Ahom (Barua 1930, p. 45). After the battle with the Naga, Sukapha organized the area into a province, putting it under the charge of *Kang-Khru-Mong*.

Sukapha then ascended the *Doi-Kao-Rong* (Patkai Hills), where he fought against the Naga of the following villages––Papuk, Tengkham, Khunkhat, Khuntung, Tangching, and Jakhang. The *Ahom Buranji* (Barua 1930) mentions the events of the battle in the following way:

> A great number of Naga were killed, and many were made captives. Some Naga were cut to pieces, and their fleshes were cooked. Then, the king made a younger brother eat the cooked flesh of his elder brother and the father of his son. Thus, Sukapha destroyed the Naga villages.

After crossing the Patkai Hills and later the Namruk River, Sukapha arrived in the Brahmaputra Valley. Here, Sukapha had to contend with the *Phu-Kao* (Moran) and the *Khan-Rang-You* (Barahi) ethnic groups who inhabited the area. However, the Ahom won over them through diplomacy and offering presents to their chiefs. In this way, Sukapha founded the Ahom kingdom or *Mong-Dun-Sun-Kham*[6] and made *Che-Tam-Doi* (Charaideo) the capital. Sukapha died in 1268 CE and was succeeded by his son Suteupha (1268 CE-1281 CE).

According to *Assam Buranji* (Phukan 1962) and the *Satsari Assam Buranji* (Bhuyan 1960), Suteupha won over the Dimasa through negotiations, which resulted in the Ahom occupation of Dimasa territory up to the *Nam-Deng* (Namdang) River. Gait (1905) also mentions Suteupha's quarrel with the Nara of Mogaung (25° 18' 00.0" N. lat. and 96° 56' 00.0" E. long.), leading the former to send an expedition against them. However, the Nara defeated the Ahom under *Phrang-Mong-Lung* (Burha-Gohain). Suteupha's son, Subinpha, succeeded him. During his reign (1281 CE-1293 CE), there is no reference to war in the chronicles. Subinpha was succeeded by his son Sukhangpha. During his reign (1293 CE-1332 CE), the Ahom fought against the *Phang* (Kamata) kingdom, which encompassed the western part of the ancient Kamarupa kingdom (Barua 1933, p. 161; Kalita 1988, p. 38; Acharyya 1966, pp. 72-73). After the skirmish, the *Kamateswar* (i.e., the Kamata king) sued for peace by giving his daughter (or sister), named Rajani, in marriage to Sukhangpha (Barua 1930, pp. 47-48). Sukhangpha's eldest son, Sukhrangpha, ascended the throne after his death. During his reign (1332 CE-1364 CE), Chao-Pulai, an Ahom prince, and *Thao-Mong-Lung* (Bar-Gohain) conspired against the monarchy. According to *Ahom Buranji* (Barua 1930), the conspirators asked Kamateswar's help, who advanced as far as Saring. However, the battle was averted through negotiation between Sukhrangpha and Kamateswar.

After Sukhrangpha died in 1364 CE, his brother Sutupha succeeded him. During his reign (1364 CE-1376 CE), the *Tiora* (Chutiya), whose kingdom lay on the north bank of the Brahmaputra River, fought against the Ahom. In fact, according to both the *Assam Buranji* (Phukan 1844) and the *Ahom Buranji* (Barua 1930), Sutupha was murdered by the Chutiya king Sankhadhvaj during a boat race. His death was followed by four years of interregnum, during which Bar-Gohain and Burha-Gohain ran the Ahom administration. Finally, in 1380 CE, Tyao-Khamti, the third son of Sukhangpha, ascended the throne. Soon after his accession, the chronicles mention that Tyao-Khamti sent an expedition against the Chutiya kingdom to avenge the murder of Sutupha (Phukan 1844, p. 14; Bhuyan 1945, p. 16). The chronicles further note that the Ahom were victorious in their campaign as the Chutiya monarch fled without resistance (Phukan 1844, p. 14; Bhuyan 1945, p. 16).

After the demise of Tyao-Khamti in 1389 CE, there was again an interregnum of eight years. Eventually, Sudangpha ascended the throne in 1397 CE. During his reign (1397 CE-1407 CE), Nara, monarch of Mogaung, named Shurunpha, sent an expedition against the Ahom kingdom under Tashenpau Bar-Gohain (Barua 1930, p. 50). According to the *Ahom Buranji* (Barua 1930), the Ahom *Chaopha* (monarch) Sudangpha marched against the invaders, fought a battle at Tipam, and defeated Tashenpau Bar-Gohain. Besides resisting the Nara invasion, the *Ahom Buranji* (Barua 1930) also mentions that Sudangpha sent an expedition against Kamateswar under Tachanbing Bar-Gohain. However, the Kamateswar averted the battle against the Ahom by seeking Sudangpha's aid to repulse the Bengal Sultan's invasion of his kingdom (Barua 1933, p. 167). Therefore, Sudangpha ordered Tachanbing Bar-Gohain to assist Kamateswar. The combined forces defeated the Sultan's contingent (Barua 1933, p. 167; Acharyya 1966, p. 80).

Sudangpha was succeeded by his son Sujanpha (1407 CE-1422 CE). The chronicles do not refer to war during his reign. The same case prevailed during Suphakpha's reign (1422 CE-1439 CE), as no battles occurred. Suphakpha's son Susenpha (1439 CE-1488 CE) ascended the throne after him. According to *Ahom Buranji* (Barua 1930), Susenpha subjugated the Naga of the Tangsu village after their rebellion. The *Buranji* further mentions that Susenpha marched with an army to battle against the Naga at Baruk. The battle resulted in the Naga's defeat. Susenpha died in 1488 CE and was succeeded by his son, Suhanpha. According to the *Assam Buranji* (Bhuyan 1930), during his reign (1488 CE-1493 CE), war with the Tangsu Naga resumed. Initially, the Naga routed an Ahom detachment, and its commander, i.e., Bar-Gohain, was killed. Hence, Nangaranga was appointed as the new Bar-Gohain, who defeated the Naga. He also captured and brought the families of Tangsu, Lephera, and Maupia to the Ahom court.

Suhanpha also fought against the Dimasa in 1490 CE. The cause, according to the *Ahom Buranji* (Barua 1930), was the construction of a fort at Tangsu village by the Ahom. The *Ahom Buranji* (Barua 1930) and the *Deodhai Assam Buranji* (Bhuyan 1932) describe the battle's events. Accordingly, the Dimasa defeated the Ahom under Khu-Na-Seng, which compelled Suhanpha to sue for peace with the Dimasa monarch by offering him a girl named Jekhring, along with two elephants and twelve enslaved people. Supimpha (1493 CE-1497 CE) ascended the throne after Suhanpha. The chronicles do not refer to any armed skirmish during his reign. He died in 1497 CE and was succeeded by his son Suhungmung (1497 CE-1539 CE).

Suhungmung had an eventful career. According to the *Ahom Buranji* (Barua 1930), the Itania Naga revolted against the Ahom in 1504 CE. Hence, Suhungmung sent an Ahom contingent under Nangaranga Bar-Gohain and Khampeng Burha-Gohain against the Naga. In the battle, the Ahom defeated the Itania Naga, and thus, the latter made peace by offering four elephants and a girl (Barua 1930, p. 54; Bhuyan 1932, p. 13). Then, in 1512 CE, Suhungmung marched with an army to Habung[7] and annexed it (Barua 1930, p. 54; Bhuyan 1932, p. 13). Next, in 1513 CE, the Ahom-Chutiya war broke out.[8] The Chutiya, led by monarch Dhitnarayan[9], marched up to *Nam-Sao* (Dikhow) River, where they fought against the Ahom, led by Suhungmung (Barpujari 1992, p. 55). In the battle, the Ahom defeated the Chutiya.

In 1520 CE, the Chutiya again invaded the Ahom territory of Mongkrang. The *Buranji* further notes that Ahom commander Khenmung tried to resist the incursion but was subsequently killed. This led the Ahom to advance to the *Ti-Phau* (Dibru) River in 1522 CE. In the ensuing armed confrontation, the Ahom defeated the Chutiya and annexed their kingdom. The Ahom put *Thao-Mong-Tiora* (Sadiya Khowa Gohain) in the conquered Chutiya territory. In 1524 CE, according to the *Deodhai Assam Buranji* (Bhuyan 1932), the Nara monarch Phuklaimung of Mogaung invaded an Ahom village named Baradeunia and killed many people. Therefore, Suhungmung sent a contingent to fight against the Nara. In a battle near Rarum, the Ahom defeated the Nara. Later, a treaty was signed between the two belligerents.

Suhungmung also fought against the Dimasa on multiple occasions. [10] For instance, Suhungmung sent an expedition under Kan-Seng against the Dimasa in 1524 CE. The Ahom were victorious, enabling them to occupy the region between *Nam-Ti-Ma* (Dhansiri) and Dikhow. Suhungmung sent a second expedition against the Dimasa in 1526 CE. In the battle, the *Buranji* mentions that the Ahom defeated the Dimasa near *Marangki* (Marangi). Suhungmung's third Dimasa expedition was sent in 1531 CE. In the following battle, the Ahom defeated the Dimasa, led by Detcha. Following that, Suhungmung installed Detchung as the new Dimasa monarch. However, in 1536 CE, Suhungmung launched a fourth expedition against the Dimasa, for Detchung showed signs of disobedience to him. In the battle, the Ahom defeated the Dimasa, killed Detchung, and occupied *Che-Din-Chi-Pen* (Dimapur), the Dimasa capital. The occupied Dimasa territory was then placed under *Thao-Mong-Marangki* (Marangi Khowa Gohain). The Dimasa, on the other hand, retreated and founded a new capital at Maibang.

Suhungmung also faced the invasion of Bengal Generals named Turbak Khan and Hussain Khan in 1532 CE. After battles on multiple fronts, the Ahom defeated Turbak Khan and Hussain Khan, and their slain heads were entombed on Charaideo Hill (Barua 1930, p. 73). Moreover, according to the *Ahom Buranji* (Barua 1930), in 1535 CE, the Naga villages of Malan, Pangkha, Khaokha, Lukna, Taru, Pahuk, Khamteng, Shiteng, and Shireng contemplated to revolt against the Ahom monarchy and thereby wanted to and seize Khamjangia Gohain. Therefore, Suhungmung despatched an expedition against the Naga, who were subsequently subdued (Bhuyan 1932, pp. 26-27).

Suhungmung was succeeded by his son Suklenmung (1539 CE-1552 CE). In 1546 CE, he faced a Koch expedition under Sukladhvaj alias Chilarai. The Koch advancing through the north bank of the Brahmaputra River reached near the *Tikarai* (Dikrai) River, where the Ahom resisted them. Both the *Ahom Buranji* (Barua 1930) and the *Deodhai Assam Buranji* (Bhuyan 1932) narrate the events of the battle between Ahom and Koch. Initially, the Ahom faced defeat at the hands of Koch, and as such, the Ahom commanders Shengkungren and Luk Hanan died while many fled and retreated to Kaliabor. But, in the next battle at Shaola, the Ahom defeated the Koch. In 1547 CE, the Ahom-Koch war resumed again. The Ahom defeated the Koch and occupied their lost territory. Then, in 1549 CE, Suklenmung sent an expedition against the Banchungia Naga to aid the Banphia Naga against the latter (Barua 1930). The Ahom defeated the Banchungia Naga and collected a war booty, including twenty buffaloes, nine wild cows, and coral beads (Barua 1930, p. 82).

After Suklenmung's death, his son Sukhampha ascended the throne. During his reign (1552 CE-1603 CE), the Ahom fought against the Naga on multiple occasions. For instance, according to the *Ahom Buranji* (Barua 1930) and the *Deodhai Assam Buranji* (Bhuyan 1932), Sukhampha sent an expedition against the Naga of Hatikhok, Iton, Papuk, and Khamteng in 1555 CE. In the battle, the chronicles mention that the Ahom defeated the Naga. Second, in 1571 CE, Naga chiefs Pungban and Pungkhru revolted against the Ahom. Hence, Sukhampha sent another expedition that subjugated the Naga (Barua 1930, p. 91). Third, in 1573 CE, the Itania Naga revolted. Hence, an Ahom expedition was sent to suppress the rebellion that subdued the Itanias (Barua 1930, p. 92). Sukhampha also faced the Bhuyans twice during his reign. First, in 1560 CE, two Bhuyan chiefs invaded the Ahom territory. The invaders encamped near the Dikhow River, where the Ahom fought a battle against them. Subsequently, the Ahom defeated the Bhuyans (Barua 1930, p. 84). Second, in 1564 CE, Sukhampha sent an expedition against the Bhela Raja, a Bhuyan chief who was defeated and captured.

Apart from the Naga and the Bhuyans, the Ahom faced the Koch multiple times during Sukhampha's reign. The war events are narrated in the *Ahom Buranji* (Barua 1930) and the *Deodhai Assam Buranji* (Bhuyan 1932). Accordingly, in 1562 CE, the Koch under Tepu and Bukutumlung reached the mouth of the Dikhow River, where a naval battle was fought against the Ahom. Again, in 1563 CE, the Koch led by Chilarai came to Dikhowmukh. The Koch were victorious in the battle. Sukhampha left his capital, *Chehung* (Garhgaon), and retreated to Klangdoi, where he remained for three months. Later, Ahom and Koch signed a treaty. Accordingly, the Koch gained territory up to Narayanpur on the north bank of the Brahmaputra River. Another Koch expedition under Tepu occurred in 1564 CE. But this time, the Ahom defeated the Koch and killed Tepu.

Besides, according to the *Ahom Buranji* (Barua 1930) and the *Deodhai Assam Buranji* (Bhuyan 1932), the Chutiya rebelled in 1564 CE. Hence, Sukhampha sent an expedition under Burha-Gohain, who defeated the Chutiya. Next, according to the *Ahom Buranji* (Barua 1930), the Nara monarch of Mogaung invaded the Ahom kingdom in 1575 CE. However, Sukhampha averted the battle by sending them gifts of one thousand gold *mohar*. Yet in 1577 CE, the Nara monarch again invaded the Ahom kingdom. Hence, Sukhampha marched against the Nara, and a battle was fought near the Sessa River. The Ahom defeated the Nara in the battle and collected a war booty (Barua 1930, p. 92; Bhuyan 1932, pp. 39-40). Susengpha (1603 CE-1641 CE) ascended the throne after Sukhampha. According to the *Ahom Buranji* (Barua 1930), during his reign (1603 CE-1641 CE), the Ahom moved to the Kapili Valley in 1606 CE, where they fought against the Dimasa on multiple fronts. Both the *Ahom Buranji* (Barua 1930) and the *Kachari Buranji* (Bhuyan 1936) narrate the events of the war.

During Susengpha's reign, the Ahom-Mughal war commenced. According to the chronicles,[11] the war broke out due to illegal activities of the Mughal merchant on the Ahom territory. The chronicles further note that the Ahom arrested some Mughal traders and confiscated their commodities. This led the Mughal *Subahdar* (governor) of Bengal, named Qasim Khan, to send an expedition against the Ahom under Syed Hakkim and Syed Aba Bakr in 1615 CE. Barpujari (1992) estimates the strength of the Mughal army to be "ten to twelve thousand cavalries and infantry, two hundred musketeers and a flotilla of three hundred or four hundred war boats." The ensuing battles that followed the Ahom by 1616 CE were able to gain the upper hand. The subsequent defeat and death of the Mughal commander Abu Bakr, notes *Baharistan-i-Ghaybi* (Borah 1936) was due to his own "negligence and arrogance," while the *Kamrupar Buranji* (Bhuyan 1930) elicits the name of the Mughal officials who surrendered to the Ahom.[12]

The *Baharistan-i-Ghaybi* (Borah 1936) also notes the casualties on the Mughal side, which stood at thousand and seven hundred men. In addition, another three thousand four hundred men who escaped the battlefront died of the wound, a thousand men were taken captive, and three thousand half-dead men concealed themselves in the jungle. Similarly, in a series of battles against another Mughal commander, Mirza Nathan, the hill Rajas of *Khamrap* (Kamrup) sought the Ahom monarch Susengpha's help, who sent an Ahom contingent of eighty thousand men under the command of Hati Baruah. After a prolonged battle, Mirza Nathan retreated to Hajo while the Ahom possessed war booty.

The Ahom-Mughal battle resumed again in 1636 CE and continued till 1639 CE. Peace between them was concluded by a treaty in 1639 CE. The treaty demarcated Barnadi on the north bank of the Brahmaputra River and Asurar Ali on the south bank of the Brahmaputra River as the boundary between the two parties (Wade 1800, p. 284; Gait 1905, p. 121). Susengpha was ascended by his eldest son, Surampha (1641 CE-1644 CE). The chronicles do not refer to any war during his reign. However, during the reign of Shuchingpha (1644 CE-1648 CE), there were two expeditions against the *Chungi* (Dafla). According to the *Assam Buranji* (Bhuyan 1945) and the *Deodhai Assam Buranji* (Bhuyan 1932), the first Ahom expedition against the Dafla occurred in 1646 CE owing to raids committed by the latter on the Ahom territory. At the same time, the second Ahom expedition took place in 1648 CE (Barua 1930). In their first expedition, the Ahom failed, but in the second expedition, the Ahom were victorious.

In 1648 CE, the nobles deposed Shuchingpha and enthroned Sutamla (1648 CE-1663 CE) to the throne. He sent two expeditions against the Lakma Naga due to raids they committed. The *Assam Buranji* (Dutta 1938) provides a detailed description of the Naga expedition. A truce was made after the submission of the Naga chiefs, who agreed to pay tribute, and in return, the Ahom offered a hill territory to the chief. Similarly, Sutamla also encountered the Miri in 1655 CE. According to the *Assam Buranji* (Dutta 1938) and the *Ahom Buranji* (Barua 1930), the Miri raided the Ahom villages by nulling the arrangement of the *posa* system, which was concluded during Susengpha's reign. Hence, Sutamla sent an expedition against the Miri. Subsequently, the Miri were defeated and were required to pay annual tribute to the Ahom (Dutta 1938, pp. 9-10).

According to the *Assam Buranji* (Dutta 1938), *Riyaz-us-Salatin* (Salim 1902), and *Maasir-i-Alamgiri* (Khan 1947), Sutamla occupied Kamrup from the Mughal *Faujdar* Lutfullah Shirazi. Hence, after the accession of Aurangzeb, Mir Jumla was appointed as the *Subahdar* (governor) of Bengal with directives to invade the Ahom kingdom (Sarkar 1916, p. 156). In the ensuing war that followed, the Ahom were defeated on multiple fronts, and in 1662 CE, Mir Jumla occupied Garhgaon, the Ahom capital (Bhuyan 1957, p. 26). However, Mir Jumla faced much hardship to retain his hold over Garhgaon and adjoining areas of Lakhau and Mathurapur due to a surprise night attack and blockade of Mughal supply lines by the Ahom (Bhuyan 1945, p. 80; Bhuyan 1957, pp. 26-28). Moreover, the advent of monsoon epidemics, such as fever and dysentery, resulted in many Mughal soldiers' deaths (Bhuyan 1957, p. 28). Thus, the chronicles[13] mention that after negotiations, a treaty was signed between Mir Jumla and Ahom[14] in 1663 CE at Ghiladharighat (Bhuyan 1957, p. 30). According to the terms of the treaty, highlighted in the *Fatiya-i-Ibriya* (Blochmann 1872):

- The Rajas of Assam and Tipam should each send one of their daughters to the imperial harem.
- Each should pay 20,000 *tolas* (1 *tola* = 0.01 kg.; 20,000 *tolas* = 233.27 kg.) of gold and 120,000 *tolas* (1399.65 kg.) of silver.
- Fifteen elephants were to be sent to the emperor, fifteen to the Nawab (Mir Jumla), and five to Dilir Khan.
- Within twelve months, 300,000 tolas (3499.14 kg.) of silver and 90 elephants will be sent as tribute to Bengal in three to four monthly installments.
- Twenty elephants are to be furnished annually.
- The sons of Budh Gosain, Karkas-ha, Bar Gosain, Parbatar, and the four principal Phukans of the Raja were to remain hostages with the Nawab until the conditions in para 4 were fulfilled.
- The following districts are to be ceded to His Majesty the Emperor–in the *Uttarkul* Sirkar Durang (Darrang), bounded by Guwahati on one side and by the Burari, which passes Fort Chamdhurah, on the other side; in *Dakhinkul*, the district of Nakirani, the Naga Hills, Beltali, Dumuria.
- All inhabitants of Kamrup who were kept as prisoners by the Raja in the hills and Namrup were to be restored, as was the family of Baduli Phukan.

As Sutamla left no heir, the nobles placed Supungmung on the Ahom throne. During his reign (1663 CE-1669 CE), the Miri raided the Ahom villages on the north bank of the Brahmaputra River in 1665 CE (Barua 1930). Hence, Supungmung sent an expedition against them. The Miri was subsequently defeated. Moreover, in 1666 CE, the *Ahom Buranji* (Barua 1930) mentioned that Supungmung also sent an expedition against the Banchangia Naga. After a brief resistance, the Naga finally surrendered to the Ahom and offered tribute to them. According to the *Assam Buranji* (Dutta 1938) and the *Kamrupar Buranji* (Bhuyan 1930), Supungmung also fought against the Mughal. After making necessary preparations,[15] the Ahom advanced towards Kamrup, attacking the Mughal garrison at Bahbari in September 1667 CE. At Bahbari, the *Kamrupar Buranji* (Bhuyan 1930) mentions that the Ahom collected war booty. Then, the Ahom proceeded towards Itakhuli, and after scaling, the fort's walls were occupied in 1667 CE. When the defeat and loss of Kamrup to the Ahom reached Aurangzeb, the Mughal Emperor, he appointed Raja Ram Singh to command an expedition in Kamrup against the Ahom (Bhattacharya 1929, p. 367). In the ensuing battles, the Ahom, after receiving an initial setback at Alaboi, triumphed over the Mughal at Saraighat in 1671 CE.

After Supungmung, his brother Sunyatpha ascended the throne. During his reign (1669 CE-1673 CE), war with the Mughal under Raja Ram Singh continued. According to the chronicles,[16] after a series of land and naval battles between the Ahom and the Mughal, Raja Ram Singh retreated to Rangamati. The chronicles also mention that Sunyatpha sent an expedition under *Phu-Ke-Lung* (Bar Barua) against the Dafla, who had raided a village and refused to pay tribute. [17] However, the Ahom expedition failed. Sunyatpha also sent an expedition against the Miri, who were defeated (Dutta 1938). The next Ahom monarch was Suklanpha (1673 CE-1675 CE). According to *Ahom Buranji* (Barua 1930), during his brief reign, an expedition was sent against the Chutiya and the Miri. Both the Chutiya and the Miri submitted to the Ahom by paying tribute. Then, between the reigns of Suhung and Sulikpha (1675 CE-1681 CE), there is no reference to any war in the chronicles. The Ahom court was filled with ministerial intrigue and conspiracy during this period.

However, during Supatpha's reign (1681 CE-1696 CE), war with the Mughal resumed. According to the *Tungkhungia Buranji* (Bhuyan 1933), Supatpha, after consulting with Burha-Gohain, Bar-Gohain, *Seng-Lung* (Barpatra Gohain), *Phu-Kan* (Phukan), and other officers, decided to attack the Mughal at Kamrup. In a series of battles that followed, the Ahom occupied Kamrup while the Mughal *Faujdar* Mansur Khan fled beyond the *Manah* (Manas) River (Bhuyan 1933, p. 17). The *Tungkhungia Buranji* (Bhuyan 1933) also mentions that the Miri killed two hundred Ahom along with the family of Sadiya Khowa Gohain. Hence, Supatpha sent an expedition under Moupia Phukan against the Miri in 1683 CE. The Miri were subjugated and had to pay tribute. Supatpha also sent two expeditions against the Naga (Bhuyan 1933, pp. 26-27). The first expedition was against the Namchang Naga, and the second was against the Naga of Doyang (Barua 1930, pp. 267-268). In both expeditions, the Ahom defeated the Naga.

Supatpha's eldest son, Sukhrungpha (1696 CE-1714 CE), ascended the throne after him. Sukhrungpha sent expeditions against the Dimasa and the *Jayta* (Jaintia). The *Tungkhungia Buranji* (Bhuyan 1933) provides a detailed description of these expeditions. The Dimasa expedition was led by Bar Barua, who marched through the Dhansiri Valley, and Pani Phukan, who marched through the Kapili Valley (Gait 1905, pp. 176-177). The expedition resulted in the Ahom occupation of Maibang, the Dimasa capital. Similarly, the Jaintia expedition was led by Bar Barua, who marched to Jaintiapur (Jaintia capital) through the Kapili Valley. In contrast, *Phu-Kan-Lung* (Bar Phukan) marched via the Jaintia Hills (Gait 1905, p. 180). The Jaintia expedition ended with the submission of the Jaintia monarch Ram Singh to Sukhrungpha. Sukhrungpha also contemplated invading Bengal, for which he raised an army (Bhuyan 1933, pp. 38-39).

Sukhrungpha was succeeded by his son Sutanpha (1714 CE-1744 CE). Gait (1905) mentions that in 1717 CE, Sutanpha sent an expedition against the Dafla, who started raiding the Ahom territory. Sutanpha died in 1744 CE and was succeeded by his brother Sunenpha, during whose reign (1744 CE-1751 CE) there was no war. After Sunenpha, Surampha (1751 CE-1769 CE) became the next monarch. In 1758 CE, the Dafla resumed their raids. The Ahom, to prevent the Dafla raids, closed the hill passes, erected forts, and allowed the Dafla to levy *posa* in the *Duar* areas (Devi 1968, p. 227). According to *Ahom Buranji* (Barua 1930), Surampha also sent an expedition against the Miri, who had stopped paying tributes. The expedition ended with Miri's surrender and offering of tribute. Besides that, according to the *Ahom Buranji* (Barua 1930) and the *Tungkhungia Buranji* (Bhuyan 1933), Surampha sent an expedition to aid Raja Jai Singh of *Magalu* (Manipur), who had been ousted from his kingdom by the monarch of *Mantara* (present-day Republic of the Union of Myanmar).

After Surampha, his brother Shunyeupha ascended the throne. His reign (1769 CE-1780 CE) was dominated by the internal rebellion against the Moamarias, Khamjania Nara, etc.[18] Then, Shuhitpangpha (1780 CE-1795 CE) ascended the throne. During his reign, the Moamaria rebellion continued (Gait 1905, p. 200). Hence, he appealed to Lumsden, the Collector of Rangpur, for aid. Lumsden sent Captain Welsh, Lieutenant Macgregor, Ensign John Peter Wade, and six companies of sixty sepoys to Goalpara in 1792 CE (Gait 1905, pp. 206-207). Captain Welsh left the Ahom kingdom in 1794 CE after suppressing the Moamarias and reinstating Shuhitpangpha at Rangpur. Suklingpha (1795 CE-1810 CE) became the next Ahom monarch. The *Tungkhungia Buranji* (Bhuyan 1933) mentions an insurrection of the Dafla during his reign. However, the Ahom were able to defeat and subjugate the Dafla. Similarly, the *Ahom Buranji* (Barua 1930) notes that in 1797 CE, the Ahom were able to defeat and suppress the combined forces of Khamti, Nara, Fakial, Miri, Misimi, Muluk, and Abor. Lastly, the *Tungkhungia Buranji* (Bhuyan 1933) notes the Ahom expedition against the Dimasa monarch Krishna Chandra. Suklingpha was succeeded by his brother Sudinpha (1810 CE-1818 CE). During his reign, the *Mon* (Burmese) invaded the Ahom kingdom in 1816 CE. The Ahom fought against the Burmese, first at Ghiladhari and later near Dihing. But the Burmese defeated the Ahom (Barua 1930, pp. 379-381).

Sudinpha was later deposed by intrigue, and in his place, Purandar Simha (1818 CE-1819 CE). was installed as the new Ahom monarch. Subsequently, the news of Sudinpha's deposition and Badanchandra's murder reached the Burmese court (Bhuyan 1933, p. 207). Hence, the Burmese again invaded the Ahom kingdom. The Ahom fought the Burmese near Nazira but were defeated. Later, the Burmese reinstated Sudinpha (1819 CE-1821 CE). as the Ahom monarch. However, he soon became indifferent toward the former. Hence, the Burmese once again invaded the Ahom kingdom. Sudinpha tried to resist the invasion but was defeated by Mingyimaha Tilowa (Lahiri 1954, p. 11). Sudinpha then left and took refuge in Bengal. The Burmese thus occupied the Brahmaputra Valley. Then, according to the *Tungkhungia Buranji* (Bhuyan 1933), the Burmese installed Jogeswar Simha as the new Ahom monarch, who ruled as a puppet.

Ahom Military Organisation

The Ahom organized their armed forces into five divisions. These were infantry, elephantry, cavalry, navy, and artillery.

Infantry

The base of the Ahom military system was the *paik-peasantry*, which Barpujari (1994) writes was "hierarchically organized and trained, ready for short notice mobilization, and backed by the entire resources and the strategic advantages of the land and the psychological sense of unity." In other words, the Ahom devised the *paik* system so that the kingdom's entire adult male population between the ages of sixteen and fifty provided compulsory military and civil services to the monarchy.

However, the Ahom royalty aristocrats, such as the three Gohains–Burha-Gohain, Bar-Gohain, and *Chao-Seng-Lung* (Barpatra-Gohain), were exempted from the service. Barpujari (1994) also opines that priests were exempted from the service. Yet, his view is not credible as both the *Ahom Buranji* (Barua 1930) and the *Satsari Assam Buranji* (Bhuyan 1960) mention that at the monarch's order, the *Deodhai Phukan* and the *Bailung Phukan*, who belonged to the priestly class fought against the Moamaria. Besides that, the *Satsari Assam Buranji* (Bhuyan 1960) notes that the monarch also ordered the *Adhikari* of the Dihing *Satra* and his followers to fight against the Moamaria.

The *paik* were organized into the lowest unit, called *kring-lang* (or *got*). The number of members included in a *got* fluctuated during the Ahom period. For example, during Sukapha's advent, a *got* comprised of three men as he brought three thousand *mo'tong-deng* (cooking pots), each serving food for three persons.[19] Thus, we can infer that three men equal one *got*. However, according to *Purani Assam Buranji* (Goswami 1922), the Ahom monarch increased the *got* to four members in the 17th century CE. Yet again, in the 19th century CE, during Surampha's reign, the *got* was reduced to three members in some areas of the kingdom (Sharma 1996, pp. 33-52). Thus, a *got* usually comprised of three to four members depending on the period and situation.

Each *got* sent one *paik* for three months a year for public works, such as building houses, roads, forts, dams, etc. At the same time, the remaining members cultivated the jointly held land, which

Sharma (1996) argues was 2.66 acres of paddy. Besides, during the battle, this *paik-peasantry* was mobilized as infantry soldiers. Thus, even without maintaining a regular paid armed force, the Ahom monarchy mobilized one-fourth of the *paik* for military usage or other activity. Meanwhile, the remaining non-serving *paik* acted as a reserved force, which, if necessary, were mobilized by officers called *kheldar* (Barpujari 1994, p. 67). The *paiks* were further grouped into a *khel* (guild) based on an occupational and territorial basis and placed under the charge of officers in a hierarchy. For example, *Ru-Sao* (Bora) commanded twenty *paik*, *Ru-Pak* (Saikia) commanded a hundred *paik*, *Ru-Ring* (Hazarika) commanded a thousand *paik*, *Phu-Kin-Mong* (Rajkhowa) commanded three thousand *paik* and *Phu-Kan* (Phukan) commanded six thousand *paik*.

However, the *paik* system began to collapse due to the loss of human resources in successive wars against many internal and external adversaries, such as the Mughal, Moamaria, etc. It eventually led to the reduction of *got* from four to three members, and according to the chronicles,[20] it also paved the way towards creating a regular force with flint guns like the Bengal sepoys during Shuhitpangpha's reign in the late 18th century CE. This regular force was made at the behest of Purnananda Buragohain by an officer named Ashan Dhanudharia Bora. It was trained by two sepoys of Captain Welsh's company, Dina and Fakirchand (Gogoi 2017, p. 39). Moreover, this force was divided into eighteen companies or divisions of sepoys, each consisting of a hundred sepoys, one *Subedar*, and two *Jamadhar*. Their attire included a *sinat-patharkalai* or flint gun, bag for keeping bullets, coat, cap, girdle, *damura* gun, pantaloons or trousers, and flag (Barua 1930, p. 358).

Nevertheless, the Ahom infantry was not only composed of *paik-peasantry* and a regularly paid force but also of armed contingent from tributary chiefs, frontier chiefs, and allied kingdoms. Evidence in the chronicles[21] shows that Sukapha was accompanied by many non-Tai people on his way to the Brahmaputra Valley. In the *Ahom Buranji*

(Barua 1930), there is a reference to a Dimasa contingent assisting the Ahom during their battle against Turbak Khan. Similarly, against the Mughal at Hajo, the Ahom were assisted by a Koch contingent of Raja Baldeva and contingents from eighteen other hill chiefs from both the banks of the Brahmaputra River (Borah 1936, p. 488).

The frontier chiefs, such as Dimarua, Hengrabari, Joy, Gukar, Manhing, Haladhibaria, Barnagaria, Kantam, Rupsing, and Bamun too, assisted the Ahom during the Ahom-Mughal war (Barua 1930, p. 106). There is also a reference in the *Jaintia Buranji* (Bhuyan 1937) that, at Supungmung's request, the Jaintia monarch sent a contingent of twenty thousand personnel to construct the rampart. Similarly, according to the *Kachari Buranji* (Bhuyan 1936), during Sukhrungpha's Dimasa expedition, the Miri ethnic group and frontier Rajas offered military service to the Ahom. Thus, the Ahom infantry was composite, comprising *paik-peasantry*, regularly paid force, and armed contingents from tributary chiefs and others.

Elephantry

Next to the infantry was elephantry. The topography of the Brahmaputra Valley is such that it facilitated the use of elephants in warfare. According to *Deodhai Assam Buranji* (Bhuyan 1932), the Ahom utilized male and female elephants during the war. The male war elephant, notes *Baharistan-i-Gayabi* (Borah 1936), "consisted of *mast* (heated) and *hushiar-mast*, i.e., elephants who have not yet come to the state of heat." The exact text further mentions that the Ahom applied *sarfil*, a herb, to a male elephant to make them *mast* within twenty-four hours.

These elephants were then actively used by the Ahom in war, and the instances are elicited in the chronicles. For example, according to the *Ahom Buranji* (Barua 1930), during the reign of Suhungmung, the Ahom utilized elephants against the Turko-Afghan at Sola, Dikaraimukh, and Bharali. Similarly, the same chronicle further mentions that the Ahom used elephants during the war against the Koch, Chutiya, Nara, and Naga. While against the Mughal at Bharali in 1616 CE, the Ahom used elephants to break enemy ramparts (Borboruah 1981, p. 97). The names of war elephants are enumerated in the *Ahom Buranji* (Barua 1930) and the *Deodhai Assam Buranji* (Bhuyan 1932). These were Pairin, Paishu, Pairak, Paikai, Khan-Ko-Mong, etc.

To maintain elephants, the Ahom monarchy installed officers of various grades. For example, *Hati-Barua*, an expert in treating elephant ailments, was put in charge of the royal elephant department. He was assisted by another officer called *Hati-Barbora*. *Hati-Kakati* was another officer who maintained records of royal elephants. Besides, the Ahom formed several guilds and utilized traditional methods, such as *Khedashikar*, *Melashikar*, etc., to capture wild elephants. One such guild, called *Hati-Chowa*, instructed the movement of wild elephants. Meanwhile, another guild, called *Hati-Sungi*, headed by *Sungi-Barua*, worked on driving the wild elephant to the rampart. Once captured, the elephants were trained in *Hati-Khok* (Bhuyan 1930, p. 84). The trained elephants were then shifted at *Hatisal*. The *maut* trained the elephants, whereas *Hati-Ghahi* maintained its sustenance.

Cavalry

The Ahom also used horses in battle along with infantry and elephantry. Evidence in the chronicles shows that Sukapha came with three hundred horses, and his successors continued the tradition of fighting on horseback. However, the significance of horses declined over the period. Barpujari (1994) provides two reasons for that—one is the topography of the Brahmaputra Valley, which, with its forests, hills, rivers, and marshes, hampers the mobility of horses; and second, the valley's climate, which was not conducive for horse breeding. Hence, to substitute the lacuna, Ahom imported *Tangan* horses from Bhutan (Gogoi 2017, p. 53).

Despite these limitations, there are multiple references in the chronicles where horses were used in battles by monarchs and commanders. For instance, during Sudangpha's reign, Ta-Chan-Bing Bar-Gohain marched on a horse to fight against the Nara (Bhuyan 1945, p. 7; Bhuyan 1960, p. 52). Likewise, Suhungmung, during his Chutiya expedition, marched on a black horse named Kansheomlan (Barua 1930, p. 56; Bhuyan 1945, p. 10). In 1546 CE, the Ahom commander, Luk Hanan, lost his life fighting against the Koch on horseback, while another commander, Daikhru, fled, leaving his horse on the battlefield (Barua 1930, p. 80). Similarly, the *Tungkhungia Buranji* (Bhuyan 1933) mentions that Debera Bar-Barua marched against Narayan Gohain of Tipam on a white pony. For the maintenance of horses, the Ahom monarchs created a separate department that supervised the royal stable, called *Ghorasal*, and it was put under the charge of an officer named *Ghora-Barua*. He was assisted by *Ghora-Barbora* (Bhuyan 1930, p. 125). Besides that, the *paik* looking after the horses were called *Ghora-Chahi*, and those supplying grass were called *Ghora-Ghahi*.

Navy

The Ahom used boats since the time of Sukapha. However, Tyao-Khamti, in the late 14th century CE, organized and strengthened the navy by constructing boats, training personnel for a naval battle, and grouping them into a new guild called *Naoboicha*, supervised by an officer *Naoboicha-Phukan*. The naval force was further reorganized by Susengpha, who divided the department into two divisions—military and civil. The military division in the western part of the kingdom was placed under *Pani-Phukan*, who was under the command of *Bar-Phukan*. Similarly, the eastern part of the kingdom was placed under *Naoboicha-Phukan*, who was under *Bar-Barua* (Gogoi 2017, p. 60). Barpujari (1994), in his work, listed varied types of boats for naval battle. Accordingly, the Ahom war boats were *Marnao, Bachari, Hilloi-Charanao*,[22] *Kusha*, and *Kush*.[23]

Regarding the boat's construction, Gogoi (2017) notes that although the Ahom designed their boats, they were also influenced by Turko-Afghan and the Mughal boats. Moreover, boats were harbored at the dockyard, and the Ahom maintained several of these in strategic locations. The Ahom developed their *Naosal* or dockyard in large swampy areas, canals, and abandoned river courses (Gogoi 2017, p. 62). The *Tungkhungia Buranji* (Bhuyan 1933) mentions the names of some dockyards. These were *Bar-Naosal* at Rangpur, *Sakbari-Naosal* at Garhgaon, *Saraibari-Naosal* at Majuli, *Negheri-Naosal* at Dergaon, and *Dighalighat-Naosal* at Jaypur. Besides these, there were also other dockyards listed by Gogoi (2017), like *Kajali-Naosal* at Kajalimukh, *Naosal* of Bharalu, Kharghuli, Dighalipukhuri and Paniphukanar at Kamrup.

The Ahom used their naval force in many battles. For instance, the *Ahom Buranji* (Barua 1930) elicits that against the Chutiya kingdom, Suhungmung sent a naval expedition under the command of Sukhring and two Railung Gohains. It further mentions that the Ahom defeated the Chutiya in the naval encounter at Dikhow and Dibru Rivers. Likewise, Suhungmung, against Turbak Khan at Sola, fielded seven hundred boats (Barua 1930). The *Baharistan-i-Ghaybi* (Borah 1936) elicits that Susengpha stationed three hundred boats at Kajali during the invasion of Sayed Abu Bakr. At Hajo against the Mughal, the Ahom fielded four thousand war boats, such as *Marnao, Bachari, Kusa, Koos*, etc. Besides, in the naval encounter against the Mughals at Saraighat in 1671 CE and Itakhuli in 1682 CE, the Ahom defeated the Mughals.

Artillery

The Ahom used both heavy and light artillery. The Ahom heavy artillery was *Klang-lung* (or *Bortop*), while the light artillery was *Klang-noi* (or *Hilloi*). Barpujari (1994) estimates that ten percent of the Ahom armed forces were experienced in using artillery, and as such, it was restricted to a few guilds, such as *Hilloidari*. Another guild-wielding firearm was created by Sukhampha in the mid-16th century CE, consisting of royal *Konwar* (prince). It was called *Konwar-Hilloidari*. This guild was further divided into two divisions based on age. The older aged division, called *Bajna-Hilloidari-Konwar*, remained under the command of *Hilloidari-Phukan*, while the younger aged division, *Bhitarual-Hilloidari-Konwar*, remained under *Hilloidari-Barua*. Apart from the guilds mentioned above, the Ahom also formulated another guild using a firearm named *Nara-Hilloidari*. The guild's members comprised the Nara ethnic group (Buragohain 2022, p. 14). Moreover, due to the effectiveness of this guild in using firearms, the Ahom monarchy employed and settled them in the Brahmaputra Valley from upper Burma (Buragohain 2022, p. 14). For further discussions on different types of Ahom artillery, its use in combat, and the officers in charge of making them, refer to chapter four.

Ahom Weapons

The Ahom, during their six hundred years reign, utilized various weapons. Based on the function, i.e., principle of operation and construction of weapon, the Ahom weapons can be grouped as melee, ranged, and defensive weapons. The Ahom melee weapon consists of edged and pointed weapons. The edged weapons were swords and choppers of several types, and the pointed weapons included spears and pikes. Concerning the ranged weapons, there were two types one based on elastic propulsion, i.e., bow and arrow, and the other based on explosive propulsion, i.e., firearm. The literature suggests that the Ahom used both heavy and light artillery. There were eleven types of light artillery and five types of heavy artillery. The defensive weapons consisted of a head cap, a thick skin jacket, and shields made of animal hide or bamboo and cane (Gogoi 2017). All these and more are vividly discussed in the following chapters.

Chapter 03

Melee Weapon

A melee weapon is a close-combat, hand-held weapon used by the user to inflict bodily harm to an opponent. The Ahom used two types of melee weapons, i.e., pointed and edged.

Pointed Weapon

Pointed weapons have sharp pointed tips designed for thrusting and penetration. Spears, pikes, etc., are some examples of pointed armaments that are effective against armored foot and mounted soldiers. Barpujari (1994), Gogoi (2006), Baishya (2009), Gogoi (2017), and Buragohain (2022) provide the names of different varieties of Ahom pointed weapons. These are *Aabor*, *Barsha* (leaf-shaped spear), *Baru*, *Duta* (javelin), *Jathi* (flat spear), *Khapor* (multi-barbed spear), *Pacha*, *Xel* (barbed spear), and *Xul* (rod spear). However, specimens of only *Jathi*, *Barsha*, and *Khapor* are found in museums across Assam.

Jathi

Jathi is a flat spear used for thrusting. It comprises a long-pointed, double-edged blade and a socket in which bamboo or a wooden shaft is inserted. The blade of the *Jathi* has a medial rib that runs from the base to the tip. Specimens of *Jathi* are preserved and displayed in two museums, namely the District Museum in Jorhat and the District Museum in Mangaldoi.

Jathi 1 (JDM/2019/85)

The *Jathi* is displayed in the District Museum in Jorhat. Its length is 89.3 cm., and it weighs 2.1 kg. The *Jathi* has a double-edged blade that tapers towards the tip. Its blade has a medial rib on both of its sides. The blade's length is 39 cm. The blade's width at its base is 6 cm., its two-third width is 5 cm., and its one-third width is 2.7 cm. The blade's cross-section is diamond. The *Jathi* also has a long tubular socket that is loosely fixed. The socket length is 15.5 cm. and its diameter is 4.4 cm. It has a pointed circular tang where the shaft was inserted. The tang length is 34.8 cm.

Jathi 2 (JDM/2019/86)

The *Jathi* is displayed in the District Museum in Jorhat. Its length is 58.2 cm., and it weighs 0.6 kg. It has a double-edged blade that tapers to a bent tip. The blade has a medial rib on both of its sides. The blade's length is 29 cm. The blade's width at its base is 5 cm., its two-third width is 3.8 cm., and its one-third width is 1.6 cm. The blade's cross-section is diamond. The *Jathi* has a long-pointed circular tang. Its tang length is 24 cm.

Jathi 3 (JDM/2019/87)

The *Jathi* is displayed in the District Museum in Jorhat. Its length is 82.5 cm., and it weighs 2.6 kg. It has a double-edged blade that tapers to a bent tip. The blade has a medial rib on both of its sides. The blade's length is 43.6 cm. The blade's width at its base is 6.5 cm., its two-third width is 6 cm., and its one-third width is 3 cm. The blade's cross-section is diamond. The *Jathi* has a long tubular socket that is loosely attached. The socket length is 21.9 cm., and its diameter is 3.3 cm. It also has a pointed circular tang. The tang length is 17 cm.

Jathi 4 (JDM/2019/88)

The *Jathi* is displayed in the District Museum in Jorhat. Its length is 67.5 cm., and it weighs 0.6 kg. It has a double-edged blade that tapers to a bent tip. The blade has a medial rib on both of its sides. The blade's length is 32 cm. The blade's width at its base is 3.9 cm., its two-third width is 3.5 cm., and its one-third width is 1.4 cm. The blade's cross-section is diamond. The *Jathi* has a tang. Its length is 26.5 cm.

Jathi 5 (JDM/2019/89)

The *Jathi* is displayed in the District Museum in Jorhat. Its length is 84.5 cm., and it weighs 2.1 kg. It has a double-edged blade that tapers towards the tip. The blade also has a medial rib on both sides. The blade's length is 39 cm. The blade's width at its base is 5.2 cm., its two-third width is 5 cm., and its one-third width is 3 cm. The blade's cross-section is diamond. The *Jathi* has a broken tubular socket. The socket length is 13 cm., and its diameter is 4.8 cm. It also has a pointed circular tang. The tang length is 32.5 cm.

Jathi 6 (JDM/2019/90)

The *Jathi* is displayed in the District Museum in Jorhat. Its length is 100.5 cm., and it weighs 2.9 kg. It has a double-edged blade that tapers towards the tip. The blade has a medial rib on both of its sides. The blade's length is 43.5 cm. The blade's width at its base is 6.5 cm., its two-third width is 6.7 cm., and its one-third width is 4 cm. The blade's cross-section is diamond. The *Jathi* has a long tubular socket. The socket length is 17 cm., and its diameter is 4.8 cm. The *Jathi* also has a pointed circular tang. However, the tang is not straight; it is curved. The tang length is 40 cm.

Jathi 7 (JDM/2019/91)

The *Jathi* is displayed in the District Museum in Jorhat. Its length is 99.5 cm., and it weighs 3.1 kg. It has a double-edged blade that tapers towards the tip. The blade has a medial rib on both of its sides. The blade's length is 43.5 cm. The blade's width at its base is 6 cm., its two-third width is 5 cm., and its one-third width is 3.7 cm. The blade's cross-section is diamond. The *Jathi* has a long tubular socket. The socket length is 17 cm., and its diameter is 4.4 cm. It has a pointed circular tang. The tang length is 39 cm.

Jathi 8 (JDM/2019/92)

The *Jathi* is displayed in the District Museum in Jorhat. Its length is 77 cm., and it weighs 1.2 kg. It has a double-edged blade that tapers towards the tip. The blade has a medial rib on both of its sides. The blade's length is 27 cm. The blade's width at its base is 4.2 cm., its two-third width is 4.5 cm., and its one-third width is 2.5 cm. The blade's cross-section is diamond. The *Jathi* has a tubular socket. The socket length is 13 cm., and its diameter is 3.8 cm. It also has a pointed circular tang. The tang length is 37 cm.

Jathi 9 (Accession No. n/a)

The *Jathi* is displayed in the District Museum in Mangaldoi. Its length is 49.1 cm. It has a double-edged blade that tapers towards the tip. The blade has a medial rib on both of its sides. The blade's length is 24.5 cm. The blade's width at its base is 3.5 cm., its two-third width is 5.3 cm., and its one-third width is 2 cm. The blade's cross-section is diamond. The *Jathi* also has a pointed tang. Its length is 24.6 cm.

Jathi 10 (DMM/AN/76/88)

The *Jathi* is displayed in the District Museum in Mangaldoi. Its length is 97.2 cm., and it weighs 2.3 kg. It has a double-edged blade that tapers towards the tip. The blade has a medial rib on both of its sides. The blade's length is 38.7 cm. The blade's width at its base is 5.5 cm., its two-third width is 5.3 cm., and its one-third width is 3.4 cm. The blade's cross-section is diamond. The *Jathi* has a tubular socket. The socket length is 12 cm. It also has a pointed circular tang. Its length is 49.7 cm.

Barsha

Barsha is a leaf-shaped spear. It has a double-edge blade and a tubular shank where the shaft was inserted. The tip of *Barsha* is acute, and it also has a medial rib. Specimens of *Barsha* are preserved and displayed in two museums, namely the District Museum in Jorhat and the District Museum in Mangaldoi.

Barsha 1 (JDM/2019/93)

The *Barsha* is displayed in the District Museum in Jorhat. Its length is 46 cm., and it weighs 0.4 kg. It has a double-edged, leaf-shaped blade that tapers to the tip. The blade's length is 30 cm. The blade's width at its base is 5.7 cm., its two-third width is 3.5 cm., and its one-third width is 1.7 cm. The blade's cross-section is lenticular. It has a long tubular shank where the shaft was inserted. The length of this part is 16 cm.

Barsha 2 (CIM: 397)

The *Barsha* is displayed in Cottage Industries Museum in Guwahati. Its length is 41 cm. It has a double-edged, leaf-shaped blade with a medial rib on both sides. The blade's length is 24.5 cm. The blade's width at its base is 3.5 cm., its two-third width is 3.9 cm., and its one-third width is 2.5 cm. The blade's cross-section is diamond. The tubular shank's length is 14 cm. and its diameter is 2.5 cm. There is also a tiny crossguard between the blade and the hollow shank. The length of the crossguard is 7.5 cm.

Barsha 3 (CIM: 361)

The *Barsha* is displayed in Cottage Industries Museum in Guwahati. Its length is 45 cm. It has a double-edged, leaf-shaped blade with a medial rib. The blade's length is 28.5 cm. The blade's width at its base is 3.5 cm., its two-third width is 3.8 cm., and its one-third width is 2.3 cm. The blade's cross-section is diamond. The tubular shank's length is 15.1 cm. and its diameter is 1.7 cm. A tiny crossguard also divides the blade and the hollow shank. The length of the crossguard is 7.5 cm.

Barsha 4 (CIM: 360)

The *Barsha* is displayed in Cottage Industries Museum in Guwahati. Its length is 41.2 cm. It has a double-edged, leaf-shaped blade with a medial rib. The blade's length is 25.5 cm. The blade's width at its base is 3 cm., its two-third width is 4 cm., and its one-third width is 2.4 cm. The blade's cross-section is diamond. The tubular shank's length is 14.1 cm. and its diameter is 2.4 cm. There is also a tiny crossguard that divides the blade from the shank. The length of the crossguard is 6.8 cm.

Khapor

Khapor is a multi-barbed spear. It has three sections––a blade, a central part with multiple barbs, and a hollow shank. The blade is leaf-shaped and double-edged. Only one specimen of *Khapor* is displayed in the Cottage Industries Museum in Guwahati.

Khapor 1 (CIM: 406)

Its full length is 73.8 cm., and its blade length is 44 cm. The blade's width at its base is 3.2 cm., its two-third width is 4 cm., and its one-third width is 3.5 cm. At the lower end of the blade, below its base, are six acute curved barbs, three on each side. The length of the first pair of barbs is 12.5 cm. The length of the second pair of barbs is 14 cm. The length of the third pair of barbs is 15.5 cm. The *Khapor* has a long tubular shank. The shank length is 17.5 cm. and its diameter is 2.3 cm.

Edged Weapon

Edged weapons have a sharp edge designed to lacerate and stab. These are effective against light-armored soldiers. Some examples of edged weapons include swords, knives, daggers, and scythes. The Ahom used two types of edged weapons sword and chopper. Swords were of two varieties, *Hengdang* and *Torowal* (Buragohain 2022, p. 17). Buragohain (2022) mentions that there were three types of *Hengdang*, such as *Deu-hengdang*, *Haat-hengdang*, and *Mantrapoot-hengdang*; while fourteen types of *Torowal*, such as *Beech-torowal*, *Borahi-torowal*, *Bijuli-torowal*, *Dutoropiya-torowal*, *Dumukhiya-torowal*, *Gupti-torowal*, *Joong-torowal*, *Jui-torowal*, *Kalika-torowal*, *Khapri-torowal*, *Lathi-torowal*, *Lora-torowal*, *Moothi-torowal*, and *Moran-torowal*.

Hengdang

A *Hengdang* is a single-edged curved sword whose blade has an upswept tip, and its long circular hilt is almost of equal length to its blade (Tripathi and Nath 2024, p. 15). It is divided into three parts blade, hilt, and scabbard. For the Ahom, *Hengdang* was a prestigious sword, as its utility was restricted to Ahom royalty and high-ranking officials (Gogoi 2006; Gogoi 2017). Often, the commanders were honored with gold and silver encrusted *Hengdang*. For instance, Lachit Barphukan was honored with a gold-encrusted *Hengdang* at the time of his appointment as the *Bar Phukan* of the Ahom forces against the Mughal (Gogoi 2017, p. 46). On the battlefield, a wielder of *Hengdang* was called *Hengdang-dhara*, and their number exceeded two hundred as Susengpha once deployed two hundred *Hengdang-dharas* to the battlefield to fight against the Mughal (Borah 1936). Such instances are also evident in the *Ahom Buranji* (Barua 1930), which states that during Turbak Khan's invasion of the Brahmaputra Valley, eight Ahom generals wielding *Hengdang* lost their lives.

However, the relevance of the *Hengdang* did not remain exclusive to military purposes as it was also used in Ahom matrimonial ceremonies. For instance, in the *chak-lang* marriage of the Ahom, the bride offers a *Hengdang* to the groom and explains the duties associated with wielding it. Gogoi (2006) states the duties as "protecting one's nation, wife, children, and dignity." Later, the groom swears by the presented *Hengdang* to eliminate evil, rule his citizens, and protect his state and religion (Gogoi 2006, p. 37). Specimens of two *Hengdang* are displayed in Assam State Museum in Guwahati, and a detailed description is provided below.

Hengdang 1 (Accession No. n/a)

The *Hengdang* length is 78 cm. It has a single-edged curved blade. The blade has an upswept tip. The blade's full length is 38.9 cm., and its ricasso length is 1.5 cm. The blade's width at its base is 2.4 cm., its two-third width is 2.5 cm., and its one-third width is 2.4 cm. The blade has a triangular cross-section. Its hilt is made out of wood and is 39.1 cm. long. Two thin cylindrical brass ferrules flank the upper and lower sections of the hilt. The hilt also has a small bud-shaped acute pommel. The hilt's cross-section is circular. The scabbard is brass-decorated and has a square end. It is made of two strips of bamboo or wood held together with either metal or rattan. A scabbard accompanies the Hengdang. Its length is 48.1 cm.

Hengdang 2 (ASM: 314)

The *Hengdang* length is 81.5 cm. It has a curved single-edged blade. The blade has an upswept tip. The blade's length is 46.5 cm., and its ricasso length is 2 cm. The blade's width at its base is 2.2 cm., its two-third width is 2.3 cm., and its one-third width is 2.1 cm. The blade has a triangular cross-section. The hilt is made out of wood and is encased with brass. The brass wrapping has many circular rings at the top and bottom sections of the hilt. The hilt length is 35 cm. The hilt has a circular cross-section.

Torowal

The Ahom *Torowal* are preserved and displayed at the District Museum in Jorhat and the Ahom-Tai Museum in Sivasagar.

Torowal 1 (JDM/2019/653)

It is displayed in the District Museum in Jorhat. Its length is 94.5 cm., and it weighs 1.1 kg. The blade is curved and single-edged and has a clip point. The blade's length is 80 cm. The blade's width at its base is 4.4 cm., its two-third width is 4.4 cm., and its one-third width is 2.3 cm. The blade's tip has a lenticular cross-section, while the remaining part has a convex cross-section. The hilt has no grip on it, which makes the tang visible. The other components of the hilt are a ferrule, a cross guard, a knuckle guard, and a small butt cap. The hilt's length is 14.5 cm. It has a rectangular cross-section. The circular ferrule is 2.4 cm. in length. The crossguard's length is 8 cm. The crossguard extends from one side to form the knuckle-guard. The full length of the knuckle-guard is 12.5 cm. Below the knuckle guard is a butt cap of 2 cm. in length.

Torowal 2 (Chamber No. 6: 50)

It is displayed in the Ahom-Tai Museum in Sivasagar. It is a curved *Torowal*, with its shape resembling the English alphabet 'S.' Its length is 92 cm. and it weighs 0.9 kg. The blade is curved and has an upswept tip. The blade's length is 80 cm., and its ricasso length is 6.4 cm. The blade's width at its base is 3.4 cm., its two-third width is 3.5 cm., and its one-third width is 3.6 cm. The blade's thin-spine part has a lenticular cross-section, while the thick-spine part has a triangular cross-section. The hilt has a wooden grip, a ferrule, a cross guard, and a knuckle guard. The hilt's length is 12 cm. The material used for grip construction is wood, and it is dark brown. The grip is straight and finely polished. The grip slightly curves at both ends before meeting the hilt's butt. The cross-section of the grip is elliptical. The mouth of the grip has a metal ferrule. The crossguard is leaf-shaped and, from one side, extends a knuckle guard while from the other side, protrudes a small, inverted, pentagonal extension. The crossguard length is 6.5 cm. and the knuckle guard length is 11.5 cm.

Torowal 3 (Chamber No. 6: 50)

It is displayed in the Ahom-Tai Museum in Sivasagar. Its length is 108 cm., and it weighs 0.8 kg. The _Torowal_ has a long and thin blade. Its length is 89 cm., and its ricasso length is 6 cm. The blade has an upswept tip. The blade's width at its base is 2.6 cm., its two-third width is 2.4 cm., and its one-third width is 2.1 cm. The blade has a triangular cross-section. Its hilt has a wooden grip with a thin metal ferrule. The grip length is 18.9 cm. The grip has a circular cross-section.

Torowal 4 (Chamber No. 6: 50)

It is displayed in the Ahom-Tai Museum in Sivasagar. Its length is 76 cm., and it weighs 0.8 kg. The _Torowal_ has a curved blade. Its length is 60.2 cm. The blade has a thick spine that tapers to an upswept tip. The blade's ricasso length is 2 cm. The width of the blade is uneven. The blade's width at its base is 4.2 cm., its two-third width is 4.1 cm., and its one-third width is 4 cm. Its hilt comprises a wooden grip, a thin ferrule, a crossguard, and a metal enclosing at its butt. The grip length is 15.8 cm. The cross-section of the grip is elliptical. The crossguard is leaf-shaped, and its length is 8.2 cm.

Torowal 5 (Chamber No. 6: 50)

It is displayed in the Ahom-Tai Museum in Sivasagar. Its length is 68.5 cm., and it weighs 0.7 kg. It has a thick spine and an upswept tip. The blade's length is 56 cm., and its ricasso length is 4 cm. The width of the blade's base is 4.2 cm., its two-third width is 4.7 cm., and its one-third width is 5.4 cm. The blade has a pentagonal cross-section. It has a hooked-shaped grip. The grip and the tang of the spine run straight only to curve at a right angle near the butt, giving the grip its distinct hook. The material used for the hilt construction is wood. Its length is 12.5 cm., and it has an elliptical cross-section. The hilt is made by attaching two pieces of wood with the tang using rivets.

Torowal 6 (Chamber No. 6: 50)

It is displayed in the Ahom-Tai Museum in Sivasagar. Its length is 82.1 cm., and it weighs 0.7 kg. It has a curved blade and an upswept tip. The blade's length is 67.5 cm. The blade's width at its base is 3.8 cm., its two-third width is 3.5 cm., and its one-third width is 3.3 cm. The blade has a triangular cross-section. The hilt is made of animal bone or horn. It comprises a grip, a brass ferrule, and an elliptical metal enclosing. The grip length is 14.6 cm., and its cross-section is elliptical. The grip runs straight only to curve at both flanks towards the butt. The ferrule has linear lines with grid patterns engraved in it.

Da or Chopper

_Da_ is a generic term used to identify and classify a wide variety of Ahom choppers. Depending on its purpose, the region it may belong to, or the name of the ethnic community who wields it, chopper's terminology is derived. Accordingly, the Ahom used chopper, such as _Bolikota-da, Khangara-da, Kopi-da, Mit-da, Mechi-da, Nakoi-da, Nara-da, Shikara-da_, etc. (Baishya 2009, pp. 304-305; Gogoi 2017, p. 48). The Ahom forged some choppers, while others were procured as tributes. For example, as tribute, _Nakoi-da_ was acquired from the Dimasa kingdom, _Shikara-da_ was received from the Miri ethnic group, and _Nara-da_ was obtained from the Aitan, Khamjang, and Tipam province (Phukan 1973, pp. 88-90). Yet once acquired, the Ahom later used the chopper in battle (Gogoi 2017, p. 47). Hence, these also constitute as Ahom weapon.

Nakoi-da

Nakoi-da is a long chopper that is either straight or curved. It is divided into two parts, blade and hilt, and its blade is almost equal in length to its hilt. The blade is slightly curved and resembles a triangle. However, the hilt is long and thin and often comprises two crossguards and a hollow tail, where a rope is tied. Specimens of *Nakoi-da* are displayed in three museums–Ahom-Tai Museum in Sivasagar, District Museum in Mangaldoi, and Assam State Museum in Guwahati.

Nakoi-da 1 (Chamber No. 6: 52)

The *Nakoi-da* is displayed in the Ahom-Tai Museum in Sivasagar. Its length is 86.3 cm., and it weighs 0.9 kg. The blade's length is 39.5 cm., and its ricasso length is 3.5 cm. The blade's width at its base is 2.5 cm., its two-third width is 3.5 cm., and its one-third width is 4.2 cm. The blade has a triangular cross-section. It has a long, thin hilt comprising a primary crossguard, a secondary crossguard, and a hollow sectioned tail. The hilt's length is 46.8 cm. The cross-section of the hilt has two distinct shapes. The cross-section between the primary and the secondary crossguard is oblong-shaped, while the cross-section between the secondary crossguard and the tail is circular. Out of the two cross guards, this *Nakoi-da* has only one brass cross guard, which is 5.4 cm. in length, whereas its secondary cross guard is broken. The tail has an elongated hollow section that is 5 cm. in length.

Nakoi-da 2 (Chamber No. 6: 52)

The *Nakoi-da* is displayed in the Ahom-Tai Museum in Sivasagar. Its full length is 91.5 cm., and it weighs 1.1 kg. The blade is incurved, and the cutting edge is on the inner side. The blade has a thick spine that gradually tapers down the tip. The blade has a drop point. The blade's length is 48.6 cm., and its ricasso length is 4.6 cm. The blade's width at its base is 2.7 cm., its two-third width is 4 cm., and its one-third width is 3.5 cm. The blade has a triangular cross-section. It has a long, thin hilt comprising a primary crossguard, a secondary crossguard, and a hollow sectioned tail. The hilt's length is 42.9 cm. The cross-section of the hilt has two distinct shapes. The cross-section between the primary and the secondary crossguard is oblong, whereas the cross-section between the secondary crossguard and the tail is circular. It also has two crossguards. The primary crossguard length is 5.3 cm., while the secondary crossguard length is 4 cm. There are two circular brass gilding at the base of both the hilt and the blade. The length of the hollow section of the tail is 5.8 cm.

Nakoi-da 3 (Chamber No. 6: 52)

The *Nakoi-da* is displayed in the Ahom-Tai Museum in Sivasagar. Its length is 116.5 cm. and it weighs 1.2 kg. The blade is incurved and triangular in design. The blade's length is 60.2 cm., and its ricasso length is 7.5 cm. The blade has a thick spine that gradually tapers down the tip. The blade's width at its base is 2.5 cm., its two-third width is 4.4 cm., and its one-third width is 4 cm. The blade has a triangular cross-section. It has a long, thin hilt comprising a primary crossguard, a secondary crossguard, and a small hollow tail. The hilt's length is 56.3 cm. The cross-section of the hilt has two distinct shapes. The cross-section between the primary and the secondary crossguard is diamond, whereas the part between the secondary crossguard and the tail is circular. There are two crossguards made of iron. The primary crossguard's length is 7.7 cm., while the secondary crossguard's length is 7.9 cm. The length of the hollow sectioned tail is 2.5 cm.

Nakoi-da 4 (Chamber No. 6: 52)

The *Nakoi-da* is displayed in the Ahom-Tai Museum in Sivasagar. Its length is 115.8 cm., and it weighs 1.5 kg. The blade is incurved and triangular in design. The blade's length is 58.5 cm., and its ricasso length is 9.5 cm. The blade has a thick spine that diminishes down the tip. The blade's width at its base is 2.5 cm., its two-third width is 3.6 cm., and its one-third width is 4.9 cm. The blade has a triangular cross-section. It has a long, thin hilt comprising a primary crossguard and a small hollow tail. The hilt's length is 57.3 cm. The cross-section of the hilt has two distinct shapes oblong and circular. The hilt has a single primary crossguard. Its length is 4.7 cm. The tail has a hollow section, and its length is 4.5 cm.

Nakoi-da 5 (Accession No. n/a)

The *Nakoi-da* is displayed in the District Museum in Mangaldoi. Its length is 102 cm. The blade is incurved and triangular in design. The blade's length is 55 cm., and its ricasso length is 3 cm. The blade's width at its base is 2.8 cm., its two-third width is 5.4 cm., and its one-third width is 2.6 cm. The blade has a triangular cross-section. It has a long, thin hilt comprising a primary crossguard, a secondary crossguard, and a hollow sectioned tail. The hilt's length is 47 cm. The hilt's cross-section has two distinct shapes. The cross-section between the primary and secondary crossguard is diamond, whereas the part between the secondary crossguard and the tail is circular. The primary crossguard is made of brass, and its length is 4.4 cm. The secondary crossguard is made of iron, and its length is 2.5 cm. One side of both the primary and secondary cross guard is broken. The length of the tail is 7 cm.

Nakoi-da 6 (Accession No. n/a)

The *Nakoi-da* is displayed in the Assam State Museum in Guwahati. Its length is 85.5 cm. The blade's length is 49.3 cm., and its ricasso length is 6.5 cm. The blade's width at its base is 2.3 cm., its two-third width is 5 cm., and its one-third width is 2.5 cm. The blade has two cross-sections. The blade's base has a diamond cross-section, while the remaining portion has a lenticular cross-section. It has a long and thin hilt comprising a primary crossguard, a secondary crossguard, and a small flat tail. The hilt's length is 36.2 cm. The hilt's cross-section has two distinct shapes. The cross-section between the primary and the secondary crossguard is diamond, whereas the part between the secondary crossguard and the tail is circular. The crossguards are made out of iron.

Nakoi-da 7 (Accession No. n/a)

The *Nakoi-da* is displayed in the Assam State Museum in Guwahati. Its length is 110.4 cm. The blade's length is 66.4 cm., and its ricasso length is 2.5 cm. The blade has a thick spine that diminishes towards the tip. The blade has a spear point. The width of the blade is uneven. The blade's width at its base is 2.4 cm., its two-third width is 3.1 cm., and its one-third width is 2.4 cm. The blade has a lenticular cross-section. It has a long hilt comprising only a secondary crossguard and a small flat tail. The hilt's length is 44 cm. The cross-section has two distinct shapes diamond and circular.

Nakoi-da 8 (Accession No. n/a)

The *Nakoi-da* is displayed in the Assam State Museum in Guwahati. Its length is 109 cm. The blade's length is 61.5 cm., and its ricasso length is 4.6 cm. The blade has a spear point. The width of the blade is uneven. The blade's width at its base is 2.5 cm., its two-third width is 3.7 cm., and its one-third width is 2.1 cm. The cross-section of the blade is lenticular. It has a long and thin hilt comprising primary and secondary crossguards. The hilt's length is 47.5 cm. The cross-section between the primary and the secondary crossguard is diamond. The primary crossguard is made out of brass. Its length is 7 cm. On the other hand, the secondary crossguard is made of iron and is 5 cm. in length.

Ahom-Dimasa Relation

As an edged weapon, *Nakoi-da* was not forged by the Ahom; instead, it was acquired as an annual tribute from the Dimasa kingdom (Phukan 1973, p. 90). But how did the Dimasa come to pay tribute to the Ahom? A discussion on the Ahom-Dimasa relation could help to answer the question.

The Dimasa kingdom flourished in the Dhansiri Valley.[24] Yet, according to the *Deodhai Assam Buranji* (Bhuyan 1932) and *Kachari Buranji*

(Bhuyan 1936), there were two branches of the Dimasa, ruling over two different parts of the Brahmaputra Valley in the 13th century CE. One branch with twelve families settled at Sadiya was ruled by Manik, and his territory extended to the Dikhow River (Kalita 1988, p. 25). At the same time, another branch dwelled between the Dikhow and Dhansiri Rivers (Kalita 1988, p. 25). This southern branch of the Dimasa traced its origin to Ghatotkach, son of Bhima and Heramba, who established their capital at Dimapur, Maibang, and later Khaspur (Bhuyan 1932, pp. 129-133). The chronicles[25] lists twelve monarchs of this southern branch.

Sukapha first encountered the Dimasa near the Namdang River, a tributary of the Dikhow River (Barpujari 1992, p. 56). But he did not fight with them. The *Ahom Buranji* (Barua 1930) states that Sukapha made an inquiry and found three thousand three hundred piers along the Namdang River from where the Dimasa used to draw water. Although Sukapha contemplated invading the Dimasa people of this region, their sheer numerical strength and organized government led him to abandon the project (Gait 1905, p. 79; Devi 1968, p. 92). Instead, Sukapha, after founding the Ahom kingdom, tried to establish a cordial relationship with the Dimasa by sending emissaries with presents, such as ten bundles of white cotton cloth and one long-neck silver water pot (Phukan *et al.* 1998, p. 26).

However, after Sukapha, a confrontation with Dimasa, though not military, occurred during Suteupha's reign, who demanded the Dimasa monarch Bicharpati Derchungpha to hand over the territory between the Dikhow and Namdang Rivers, otherwise to pay tribute (Barpujari 1992, p. 56; Devi 1968, p. 93). Instead of a battle, *Satsari Assam Buranji* (Bhuyan 1960) mentions that both parties decided to settle the dispute through negotiation. Thus, an understanding was met, leading the Dimasa to give up territory to the Namdang River. Hence, by the end of the 13th century CE, the Namdang River became the boundary between the two kingdoms.

Yet after this settlement, the Ahom-Dimasa battle broke out in 1490 CE during Suhanpha's reign. According to the *Ahom Buranji* (Barua 1930), the Ahom constructed a fort at Tangsu village on the upper banks of the Dikhow River, which led the Dimasa to commit armed aggression against the Ahom. Both the *Ahom Buranji* (Barua 1930) and the *Deodhai Assam Buranji* (Bhuyan 1932) provide an account of the ensuing battle where the Dimasa massacred an Ahom contingent of one hundred and twenty soldiers along with their commander Khu-Na-Seng. This defeat compelled Suhanpha to make peace with the Dimasa monarch by offering a girl with two elephants and twelve enslaved women (Barua 1930, p. 53; Bhuyan 1932, p. 12; Bhuyan 1960, p. 12).

Confrontation with the Dimasa started again during Suhungmung's reign. Suhungmung, after his victory over the Chutiya kingdom in 1523 CE, wanted to expand the Ahom territory west of the Dikhow River (Devi 1968, p. 95; Barpujari 1992, p. 58). On the other hand, the Dimasa also encroached and raided villages in the Ahom territory (Barua 1930, p. 58). Hence, Suhungmung sent an expedition against the Dimasa under Kan-Seng in 1524 CE (Bhuyan 1936, p. 11). The Ahom defeated the Dimasa on multiple fronts, pushing them back as far as *Marangki* (Marangi) and thereby claiming Dergaon (Devi 1968, p. 95). However, the Dimasa refused to cede Dergaon, which led the Ahom to resort to diplomatic negotiation. Finally, the Dimasa withdrew from Dergaon, ceding the territories west of Dhansiri River (Barpujari 1992, p. 58). The Ahom, thus, occupied the region between the Rivers Dikhow and Dhansiri.

Later, in 1526 CE, according to the *Ahom Buranji* (Barua 1930), the Dimasa again crept into the Ahom territory. This led to the renewal of the Ahom-Dimasa war. In the ensuing battle, the Ahom defeated the Dimasa near Marangi (Bhuyan 1945, pp. 11-12). Again, in 1531 CE, the Ahom-Dimasa battle resumed, and the Dimasa, led by Detcha (Dimasa monarch Khunkhara's brother), attacked Marangi.

The Ahom killed Detcha and collected a war booty, including swords (Devi 1968, p. 98). Yet, the battle continued. Finally, the Ahom army captured Dimapur, crowned Detchung as the new Dimasa monarch, and designated him "established and preserved." Henceforth, the Dimasa monarchs paid an annual tribute to the Ahom, which, according to the *Assam Buranji* (Bhuyan 1945), included *Nakoi-da*, among other articles.

Shikara-da

Shikara-da (also known as *Miri-da*) is a chopper with a curved blade, truncated tip, and round wooden hilt. The Ahom acquired *Shikara-da* as a tribute and war booty from the Miri ethnic group (Devi 1968; Phukan 1973). Only one specimen of *Shikara-da* is displayed in the District Museum in Mangaldoi.

Shikara-da 1 (DMM/AN/133/91)

Its full length is 66.5 cm. It has a curved blade, and the thickness of the spine diminishes towards the tip. As a result, the blade has a truncated tip. The blade's full length is 49 cm., and its ricasso length is 1.7 cm. The blade's width at its base is 3.5 cm., its two-third width is 3 cm., and its one-third width is 6 cm. Its hilt has two parts a wooden grip and a ferrule. The hilt's length is 17.5 cm. The ferrule length is 2.7 cm. The grip's cross-section is circular.

Ahom-Miri Relation

Like *Nakoi-da* was obtained from the Dimasa kingdom, the Ahom received *Shikara-da* as an annual tribute from the Miri ethnic group (Phukan 1973, p. 89). The Miri (also known as Mishing) lived on the plain and lower hill along the northern bank of the Brahmaputra Valley, stretching from the Subansiri River on the west to the Dihong River on the east (Devi 1968, p. 197). The Ahom annexation of the Chutiya kingdom in 1523 CE led to the occupation of the territory up to the Subansiri River. This brought them in direct contact with the Miri. The first Ahom monarch to establish diplomatic relations with the Miri was Susengpha. The chronicles note the appointment of *Chao-Tang*[26] or *Kataki*, i.e., court messengers or royal ambassadors entrusted to supervise the Miri and report if they committed any raid. Moreover, Susengpha, to check the incursion of the Miri, also introduced the *Posa* system,[27] which granted the Miri to levy and collect annual tax from specific villages in the plain in return for paying a yearly tribute to the Ahom monarchy (Devi 1968, p. 200). Thus, the Ahom compelled the Miri to accept their suzerainty.

Yet it did not refrain the Miri from raiding the villages in the plain. Sutamla had to encounter the Miri in 1655 CE (Gohain 1942, p. 135; Gait 1905, p. 128). Both the *Assam Buranji* (Dutta 1938) and the *Ahom Buranji* (Barua 1930) state that the Miri, nulling the arrangement of the *Posa* system, raided Ahom villages. This led Sutamla to retaliate by sending an armed contingent against them. The Miri were subsequently defeated. As compensation for raids, the Miri paid tributes which the *Assam Buranji* (Dutta 1938) and the *Ahom Buranji* (Barua 1930) mention, included twelve Miri people, thirty *methons* (wild cows), thirty *goru* (cows), twenty *pohumora kukur* (hunting dogs), five *paat khiya moni* (wreaths of jewels), twenty *jim-kaapor* (Miri blankets) and twenty *Shikara-da*. In addition to this, the chronicle states that Miri also agreed to pay an annual tribute of eight wild cows, twenty hunting dogs (hunting dogs do not appear in the *Ahom Buranji*), five wreaths of jewels, twenty Miri blankets, horses (the *Assam Buranji* does not refer to horses) and twenty *Shikara-da*.[28] After this settlement, Sutamla, impressed by the martial abilities, employed Miri as a soldier in the Ahom army (Devi 1968, p. 203).

According to the *Ahom Buranji* (Barua 1930), in 1665 CE, during the reign of Supungmung, the Miri once again plundered the villages on the north bank of the Brahmaputra River. An expedition was, thus, sent against the Miri, who were defeated and, therefore, came to terms with the Ahom. The next expedition against the Miri occurred during Sunyatpha (Dutta 1938, p. 32). The chronicles, however, do not provide the cause of the expedition. Therefore, Devi's (1968) account has been considered who suggests the reason for the expedition in the following lines:

> It seems that King Udayaditya Singh sent the expedition against the Miri, who had committed a raid during the reign of his predecessor, and it was most probably sent on account of the fact that this Miri, in spite of the devastation caused to their territory by the Ahom army sent by King Chakradhvaj Singh did not make their submission and conclude peace with the Ahom king.

Subsequently, the Miri were defeated and had to submit before the Ahom monarch, and as such, they offered many articles to the Ahom, including *Shikara-da*. The next Ahom monarch to send an expedition against the Miri in 1683 CE was Supatpha. The cause of the campaign, as corroborated in the *Tungkhungia Buranji* (Bhuyan 1933) and the *Ahom Buranji* (Barua 1930), was the massacre of two hundred Ahom citizens, including the death of Sadiya Khowa Gohain (Ahom governor of Sadiya), and burning of his house. Moupia Phukan, who was put in charge of the expedition, suppressed the Miri and collected a substantial amount of war booty that the chronicle mentions,[29] included large quantities of *Shikara-da*, wild cows, copper vessels, and other articles. Thus, from the discussion, it is evident that the Ahom acquired *Shikara-da* not just as tributes but also as war booty from the Miri.

Chapter 04

Ranged Weapon

A ranged weapon is a long-range assault weapon that is either hand-held or supported and is used by the user to inflict harm on a person or object. The Ahom used two types of ranged weapons: one was based on explosive propulsion, i.e., firearm, and the other was based on elastic propulsion, i.e., bow and arrow.

Firearm

There is ambiguity among scholars regarding the earliest usage of firearms by the Ahom. Wade (1800), in his book *An Account of Assam*, suggests that firearms came to be used by the Ahom after Turbak Khan's invasion in 1532 CE. Accordingly, the Ahom craftsmen began to manufacture "muskets" by copying the cannons brought by Turbak from Bengal. Gait (1905) also holds the same view in his book *A History of Assam*. He opines that "cannon, matchlock, and gun" were introduced to the Ahom by the invading generals from Bengal, such as Bar Uzir and Turbak, in 1527 CE and 1532 CE, respectively. He further argues that the Ahom weapons consisted of swords, spears, and bows and arrows before this date.

However, the views of Wade (1800) and Gait (1905) are refuted by Borboruah (1981) in his book *Ahomar Din*. He argues that the acquisition and introduction of *Mithaholong* (a type of cannon) among the Ahom started after Chutiya's defeat against the former in 1523 CE. Baruah (1985), in her book *A Comprehensive History of*

Assam, held the same view and wrote that before Turbak's invasion in 1532 CE, the Ahom monarch Suhungmung fought against the Chutiya, and after the latter's defeat in 1523 CE, the Ahom obtained "firearm" from them. Barpujari (1994) also upholds the same view in his book *The Comprehensive History of Assam*. He argues that after 1523 CE, Suhungmung commenced the manufacture of cannons.

Laichen (2003), in his article *Military Technology Transfer from Ming China and the Emergence of Northern Mainland Southeast Asia*, also writes against the conventional view of firearms introduction among the Ahom in 1527 CE or 1532 CE. He infers from the chronicles that after subjugating the Chutiya in 1523 CE, the Ahom procured "cannon" from them. Thus, based on the above inference, Gogoi (2006), in his article *War Weapons in Medieval Assam* reasons that Chutiya knew the usage of cannon before their war with the Ahom in 1523 CE, and from the war's outcome, he deduces that the Ahom must have used "cannon" in the battle against the Chutiya or else it would be impossible for the Ahom to win the war using less effective weapons, such as bow and arrow.

Yet how far are these views legitimate, i.e., are these views at par with the chronicles? Let us delve into what the chronicles have to say about the utility of firearms among the Ahom. The earliest reference to the firearm is found in the *Kachari Buranji* (Bhuyan 1936), which states that the Ahom defeated the Dimasa and obtained *Hilloi, Baru, Barsha*, etc., in 1473 CE. Likewise, *Deodhai Assam Buranji* (Bhuyan 1932), *Assam Buranji* (Bhuyan 1945), and *Satsari Assam Buranji* (Bhuyan 1960) mention that the Ahom, defeating the Chutiya in 1523 CE, collected firearms.[30]

Then, in the *Ahom Buranji* (Barua 1930), there is a reference to the Ahom-Dimasa battle in 1531 CE. In the battle, the chronicle mentions that the Dimasa lost and had to surrender *Bortop* (large cannon) and other articles to the Ahom. Similarly, the *Ahom Buranji* (Barua 1930) and the *Deodhai Assam Buranji* (Bhuyan 1932) mention that after the defeat of the Turko-Afghan, such as Nawab Bit Manik and Bar Ujir in 1527 CE, and Turbak Khan in 1532 CE, the Ahom collected many *Hilloi* and *Bortop* from them.

From the above details furnished in the chronicles, it is evident that the Chutiya and the Dimasa owned firearms in the early 16th century CE. And that they were using it in combat against the Ahom. Besides, it is also unreasonable to think of the Ahom winning battle after battle against adversaries possessing firearms, such as Chutiya, Dimasa, and later Turko-Afghan, with solely edged and pointed weapons. They must have used firearms in these battles, or the outcome wouldn't favor the Ahom. Based on this reasoning, it is argued that the Ahom knew the craft of making and using firearms before the earliest reference in the chronicles, i.e., 1473 CE (Bhuyan 1936, p. 11). Thus, Gait's (1905) remark that the Ahom started using firearms since Turbak's invasion in 1532 CE needs to be rebuked. However, it is undeniable that the Ahom learned the utility of novel firearms from their adversaries. For example, the Ahom learned the utility of the *Mithaholong* cannon from the Chutiya and *Tubuki* from the Mughal.

Considering the firearm department, Gogoi (2017) suggests that its organization started during Suhungmung's reign. But the question is why during Suhungmung's reign, why not before him? The reason is that during Suhungmung's reign, the Ahom kingdom expanded to areas rich in mineral resources, including iron ore; second was the foreign invasion, such as from the Turko-Afghan; and third was the migration of Chutiya artisans to Ahom territory, which facilitated the creation and organization of firearm department. Saltpetre and sulphur were required to create gunpowder, and for its procurement and preparation, the Ahom monarchy created separate guilds. One called *Khargharia* was engaged in manufacturing *Khar* or gunpowder. *Khargharia-Phukan* and *Khargharia-Barua* supervised it. The gunpowder was stored in *Kharbhandari*, at Garhgaon, Rangpur, Kaliabor, etc.

There was also another guild called *Jakharia* that was engaged in manufacturing saltpetre. Saltpetre was once manufactured in the present-day Shilakuti-Bajni near Sivasagar and Khargaria Daba near Moran (Buragohain 2022, p. 12). Phukan (1973) mentions that there were three ways of obtaining saltpetre. One was from cow urine, the second from bat dung, and the third from banana ashes. The third guild, called *Gandhia*, was engaged in producing sulphur. That the Ahom produced gunpowder in large quantity can be realized from the fact that Mir Jumla, who invaded the Ahom kingdom in 1662 CE, collected a war booty including three hundred forty *maund* of gunpowder (equivalent to 12690.22 kg.) (Sarkar 1951, p. 248). While about the quality of Ahom-made gunpowder, the *Fatiya-i-Ibriya* (Sarkar 1915) mentions, "They (the Ahom) make first rate gunpowder of which they procure the materials from the imperial dominions." Similarly, Tavernier also praises the Ahom gunpowder, saying, "Iron guns and the gunpowder made in that country (Ahom kingdom) is excellent."[31]

So forth, discussion is made on the genesis of firearms and its organization among the Ahom. Yet, who was using the firearm remains to be discussed. Barpujari (1994) argues that firearm usage among the Ahom soldiers was limited and not accessible to all; as such, initially, there was only one guild called *Hilloidhari* experienced in using firearms. Later, according to *Tungkhungia Buranji* (Bhuyan 1933), Sukhampha, in the 16th century CE, created another firearm-wielding guild called *Hilloidhari-Konwar* entrusted to protect the royal palace and its enclosures, the capital and its surroundings. This guild comprising Ahom princes was further divided into two groups based on age–the older, i.e., *Bajua-Hilloidhari-Konwar*, was under *Hilloidhari-Phukan*, whereas the younger, i.e., *Bhitarual-Hilloidhari-Konwar*, was under *Hilloidhari-Barua* (Bhuyan 1933, p. 241; Barpujari 1994, p. 74).[32]

However, realizing the importance of firearms in wars against adversaries, such as the Mughal and others, the Ahom monarchy increased the firearm-wielding guilds. These new guilds were organized based on ethnic groups (e.g., *Nara-Hilloidhari*), place (e.g., *Athganya-Hilloidhari*), assigned duty (e.g., *Gandhiagharia-Hilloidhari*), wielded firearm (e.g., *Bar-Hilloidhari, Maju-Hilloidhari, Haru-Hilloidhari, Gathiajamuri-Hilloidhari, Pahlangi-Hilloidhari,* etc.).

Now, speaking of the different variety of firearms, these can be classified into three types, such as:

i. *Klang-lung* (or *Bortop*)–the literature suggests five types of *Bortop*, such as *Baghmura-bortop, Biagom-bortop, Hatimuria-bortop, Mithaholong-bortop*, and *Tubuki-bortop*. These were often installed at the entrance or corners of the fortress and palace, such as at Karenghar, Paniduar, Simhaduar, Barduar, etc. (Buragohain 2022, p. 13).

ii. *Klang-noi* (or *Hilloi*)–according to literatures, there were twelve types of *Hilloi*, such as *Bachadari-hilloi, Chowa-hilloi, Gathia-hilloi, Jambur-hilloi, Jumur-hilloi, Kachai-hilloi, Kamayan-hilloi, Khoka-hilloi, Pani-hilloi, Pohulguri-hilloi, Ramchangi-hilloi*, and *Saru-hatnalia-hilloi*.

iii. *Chandraban*–the *Baharistan-i-Gayabi* (Borah 1936) mentions that the Ahom used a *Chandraban* rocket.

Along with the firearms mentioned above, the Ahom also, from time to time, obtained firearms as war booty from the Turko-Afghan, Dimasa, Chutiya, and Mughal. In fact, Gogoi (2017) suggests that Ahom did not just use the acquired firearms in war, but these also influenced the design and shape of Ahom firearms. For instance, there is a similarity in names between Ahom and Mughal firearms, such as the term *Jambur*, a type of *Hilloi*, originates from the Mughal-made *Zambur* (Barpujari 1994, p. 73).

Bortop

Bortop is a generic term used to describe a wide variety of Ahom heavy artillery or cannon. It comprises a barrel with a vent and a muzzle, a handle behind the breech base with a knob, and a stand attached to the trunnion. Specimens of *Bortop* are preserved and displayed in the premises of Talatalghar in Sivasagar, District Museum in Jorhat, District Museum in Dibrugarh, Ahom Tai Museum in Sivasagar, District Museum in Tezpur, and Assam State Museum in Guwahati.

<u>*Bortop 1*</u>

The cannon is displayed on Talatalghar's premises in Sivasagar. It is called *Nag-Bortop*, for its muzzle resembles a serpent's hood. The cannon has an inscription where the words Sri Swarganarayan Baradaya Diyasimha and the date 1771 CE are legible (Buragohain 2022, p. 22). Its total length is 410 cm., and its barrel length is 266 cm. The barrel has a blocked vent, and its diameter is 2 cm. The cannon has two trunnions. Each length is 13 cm. and their diameter is 8 cm. The muzzle's external diameter is 42 cm., and the bore diameter is 12 cm. The breech's external diameter is 54 cm. The distance between vent to muzzle is 162 cm., vent to breech base is 13.5 cm., trunnion to muzzle is 134 cm., and trunnion to breech base is 120 cm. The cannon has a long handle. Its length is 140 cm. The handle also has a knob. The knob length is 14.5 cm., and the circumference is 62 cm.

<u>*Bortop 2*</u>

The cannon is displayed on Talatalghar's premises in Sivasagar. It is called *Hatimuria-Bortop* as its muzzle's circumference is equivalent to the size of an elephant's head. The cannon has an inscription, and its legible part mentions that Bohikhowa Barphukan made the cannon at Garhgaon and presented it to Monarch Surampha. According to oral tradition, the range of the cannon is 24 km. (15 mi.) (Buragohain 2022, p. 8). Its total length is 555 cm., and its barrel length is 380 cm. The barrel has a blocked vent, and its diameter is

1.5 cm. The tradition suggests that the British blocked the cannon's vent to prevent its use. The cannon has six trunnions. Its length is 18 cm., and its average diameter is 8 cm. The muzzle's external diameter is 62.5 cm., and the bore diameter is 17 cm. The breech's external diameter is 47 cm. The distance between vent to muzzle is 365 cm., vent to breech base is 15 cm., trunnion to muzzle is 285 cm., and trunnion to breech base is 92 cm. The cannon has a long handle. Its length is 160 cm. The handle also has a knob. The knob length is 14.5 cm., and the circumference is 58 cm.

Bortop 3

The cannon is displayed on Talatalghar's premises in Sivasagar. It is called *Hatikhujia-Bortop* as its muzzle's circumference is equivalent to the size of an elephant's foot. The cannon has an inscription. Accordingly, Gondia Goria made this cannon at Kharguli, near present-day Guwahati, under orders from Handique Barphukan and presented it to Supatpha (Buragohain 2022, p. 21). Its total length is 426 cm., and its barrel length is 300 cm. The barrel has a blocked vent, and its diameter is 2.5 cm. Just like the previous cannon, tradition tells that the British also blocked its vent as a preventive measure against any future use. The trunnion length is 18 cm., and the diameter is 7.5 cm. According to oral tradition, the cannon's muzzle has a floral and leaf-shaped design, which has gold gilding that the British looted. The muzzle's external diameter is 39.5 cm., and the bore diameter is 10 cm. The breech's external diameter is 57 cm. The distance between vent to muzzle is 288 cm., vent to breech base is 10 cm., trunnion to muzzle is 173 cm., and trunnion to breech base is 125 cm. The cannon has a long handle. Its length is 118 cm. The handle also has a knob. The knob length is 14 cm., and the circumference is 46 cm.

Bortop 4

The cannon is displayed on Talatalghar's premises in Sivasagar. It is a *Nag-Bortop* with an inscription whose only names, Gadadhar

Simha, Guwahati, and Sri Swarganarayan, are legible. Its total length is 350 cm., and its barrel length is 223.5 cm. The barrel has a blocked vent, and its diameter is 2 cm. The trunnion length is 10 cm., and the diameter is 6 cm. The muzzle's external diameter is 28 cm., and the bore diameter is 9.5 cm. The breech's external diameter is 32 cm. The distance between vent to muzzle is 214 cm., vent to breech base is 7.5 cm., trunnion to muzzle is 136 cm., and trunnion to breech base is 92 cm. The cannon has a handle. Its length is 120 cm. The handle also has a knob. The knob length is 13.5 cm., and the circumference is 40 cm.

Bortop 5

The cannon is displayed on Talatalghar's premises in Sivasagar. It is a *Hatikhujia-Bortop*, and it has an inscription that is not legible. Its total length is 350 cm., and its barrel length is 255 cm. The barrel has a blocked vent, and its diameter is 1.5 cm. The trunnion length is 10 cm., and the diameter is 5 cm. The muzzle's external diameter is 37.5 cm., and the bore diameter is 9 cm. The breech's external diameter is 50 cm. The distance between vent to muzzle is 245 cm., vent to breech base is 9 cm., trunnion to muzzle is 137 cm., and trunnion to breech base is 115 cm. The cannon's handle length is 90 cm. and it also has a knob. The knob length is 16 cm., and its circumference is 47 cm.

Bortop 6 (Accession No. n/a)

The cannon is displayed at the the District Museum in Jorhat. Its total length is 175 cm., and its barrel length is 160 cm. The barrel has a blocked vent, and its diameter is 2 cm. The cannon's muzzle has a human face engraved in it. Two distinct eyes with eyebrows and a prudent nose are visible. The muzzle's external diameter is 14 cm., and the bore diameter is 6.5 cm. The breech's external diameter is 20 cm. The distance between the vent and to muzzle is 156 cm., and between the vent and the breech base is 3 cm. The cannon has a broken handle behind the breech. Its length is 11 cm. while its circumference is 22 cm.

Bortop 7 (Accession No. n/a)

The cannon is displayed at the District Museum in Jorhat. Its total length is 149 cm., and its barrel length is 131 cm. The barrel has a blocked vent, and its diameter is 2.5 cm. The cannon's trunnions are broken. The muzzle's external diameter is 13.5 cm., and the bore diameter is 6 cm. The breech's external diameter is 20 cm. The distance between vent to muzzle is 126 cm., vent to breech base is 7 cm., trunnion to muzzle is 71 cm., and trunnion to breech base is 60 cm. The cannon has a broken handle behind the breech. Its length is 11 cm., while its circumference is 22.5 cm.

Bortop 8 (DMD/199/94/1)

The cannon is displayed at the District Museum in Dibrugarh. Its total length is 177 cm., and its barrel length is 143 cm. The cannon has trunnions, and attached to it is a stand. The trunnion length is 8.5 cm., and its diameter is 4 cm. The stand length is 48 cm. The vent diameter is 4 cm. The cannon's muzzle has a human face engraved in it. Two distinct eyes with eyebrows and a prudent nose are visible. The muzzle's external diameter is 7.5 cm., and the bore diameter is 6.5 cm. The breech's external diameter is 25 cm. The distance between vent to muzzle is 137 cm., vent to breech base is 4 cm., trunnion to muzzle is 93 cm. and trunnion to breech base is 49.5 cm. The cannon has a handle and is 34 cm in length.

Bortop 9 (Accession No. n/a)

In the Ahom Tai Museum, a cannon's barrel is on display. The barrel is 258 cm. long, and its external diameter is 6 cm. The barrel is damaged and rusted. It has a trunnion, the length of which is 5 cm., and the diameter is 2 cm. The bore diameter is 4 cm. The distance between the trunnion and the muzzle is 127 cm.

Bortop 10 (DMT: 184)

The cannon is displayed at the premises of the District Museum in Tezpur. Its total length is 197 cm., and its barrel length is 126 cm. The barrel has four rings. The cannon also has trunnions, and attached to it is a stand. The trunnion length is 4 cm., and its diameter is 2 cm. The strand length is 37 cm. The vent diameter is 0.5 cm. The muzzle's external diameter is 12 cm., and the bore diameter is 5 cm. The breech's external diameter is 18 cm. The distance between vent to muzzle is 123.5 cm., vent to breech base is 2 cm., trunnion to muzzle is 78 cm. and trunnion to breech base is 48 cm. The cannon has a long handle behind the breech. Its length is 68 cm. The handle also has a knob. The knob length is 1.5 cm, and its circumference is 14.5 cm.

Bortop 11 (DMT: 185)

The cannon is displayed at the premises of the District Museum in Tezpur. Its total length is 120 cm. The cannon's barrel has nine circular rings. The muzzle's external diameter is 18 cm., and the bore diameter is 9 cm.

Bortop 12 (DMT: 186)

The cannon is displayed at the premises of the District Museum in Tezpur. Its total length is 124.5 cm. The cannon's barrel has ten circular rings. The muzzle's external diameter is 15.5 cm., and the bore diameter is 8.5 cm.

Bortop 13 (DMT: 187)

The cannon is displayed at the premises of the District Museum in Tezpur. Its total length is 122.5 cm. The cannon's barrel has nine circular rings. The muzzle's external diameter is 17 cm., and the bore diameter is 8.5 cm.

Bortop 14 (DMT: 188)

The cannon is displayed at the premises of the District Museum in Tezpur. Its total length is 116.5 cm. The cannon's barrel has nine circular rings. The muzzle's external diameter is 18 cm., and the bore diameter is 8.4 cm.

Bortop 15 (DMT: 189)

The cannon is displayed at the premises of the District Museum in Tezpur. Its total length is 123 cm. The cannon's barrel has nine circular rings. The muzzle's external diameter is 18 cm., and the bore diameter is 10.5 cm.

Bortop 16 (DMT: 190)

The cannon is displayed at the premises of the District Museum in Tezpur. Its total length is 112 cm., and its barrel length is 90 cm. The barrel has four rings. The cannon has trunnions. Their length is 8 cm. each, and the diameter is 4.5 cm. The vent diameter is 1 cm. The muzzle's external diameter is 25 cm., and the bore diameter is 9 cm. The breech's external diameter is 23 cm. The distance between vent to muzzle is 85 cm., vent to breech base is 5.5 cm., trunnion to muzzle is 48 cm. and trunnion to breech base is 42 cm. The cannon has a broken handle. Its length is 19 cm.

Bortop 17 (ASM: 274)

The cannon is displayed at Assam State Museum in Guwahati. The cannon has an inscription in which the name of the Ahom monarch Gadadhar Simha, along with the date 1604 Saka, i.e., 1682 CE, is inscribed. Its total length is 144 cm., and its barrel length is 120.5 cm. The barrel has four rings. The trunnion length is 7.5 cm., and its diameter is 5.5 cm. The vent diameter is 2 cm. The muzzle's external diameter is 15 cm., and the bore diameter is 6 cm. The breech's external diameter is 26.5 cm. The distance between vent to muzzle is 120 cm., vent to breech base is 6 cm., trunnion to muzzle is 66.5 cm. and trunnion to breech base is 58 cm. The cannon has a knob behind the breech. The knob length is 9.5 cm., and its circumference is 23.5 cm.

Bortop 18 (ASM: 275)

The cannon is displayed at Assam State Museum in Guwahati. The cannon has an inscription in which the name of the Ahom monarch Gadadhar Simha and the date 1604 Saka, i.e., 1682 CE, is inscribed. Its total length is 145 cm., and its barrel length is 124 cm. The barrel has three rings. The trunnion length is 8.5 cm., and its diameter is 6 cm. The vent diameter is 0.4 cm. The muzzle's external diameter is 13 cm., and the bore diameter is 6.5 cm. The breech's external diameter is 20 cm. The distance between vent to muzzle is 120.5 cm., vent to breech base is 6 cm., trunnion to muzzle is 78.5 cm. and trunnion to breech base is 48 cm. The cannon has a knob behind the breech. The knob length is 11.5 cm., and its circumference is 24 cm.

Bortop 19 (ASM: 276)

The cannon is displayed at Assam State Museum in Guwahati. The cannon has an inscription in the Sanskrit language where the name of the Ahom monarch, Gadadhar Simha, and his victory over the Mughal, along with the date 1604 Saka, i.e., 1682 CE, is inscribed. Its total length is 134.5 cm., and its barrel length is 118.5 cm. The trunnion length is 5.5 cm., and its diameter is 5 cm. The vent diameter is 1.5 cm. The cannon's muzzle has a human face engraved in it. Two distinct round eyes and a prudent nose are visible. The muzzle's external diameter is 11.5 cm., and the bore diameter is 6.5 cm. The breech's external diameter is 17 cm. The distance between vent to muzzle is 113.5 cm., vent to breech base is 14 cm., trunnion to muzzle is 72 cm. and trunnion to breech base is 58 cm.

Bortop 20 (ASM: 275/284)

The cannon is displayed at Assam State Museum in Guwahati. The cannon has an inscription in Sanskrit and Persian, where the name of the Ahom monarch Gadadhar Simha and the date 1604 Saka, i.e., 1682 CE, is inscribed. Its total length is 112 cm., and its barrel length is 104 cm. The trunnion length is 7 cm., and its diameter is 3.5 cm. The vent diameter is 0.3 cm. The muzzle's external diameter is 9.5 cm., and the bore diameter is 4.3 cm. The breech's external diameter is 15 cm. The distance between vent to muzzle is 99.5 cm., vent to breech base is 7 cm., trunnion to muzzle is 63.5 cm. and trunnion to breech base is 43 cm.

Bortop 21 (ASM: 295)

The cannon is displayed at Assam State Museum in Guwahati. Its total length is 330 cm., and its barrel length is 268 cm. The trunnion length is 14.5 cm., and its diameter is 7.5 cm. The vent diameter is 1 cm. The muzzle's external diameter is 33.5 cm., and the bore diameter is 8 cm. The breech's external diameter is 35 cm. The distance between vent to muzzle is 256 cm., vent to breech base is 15 cm., trunnion to muzzle is 164 cm. and trunnion to breech base is 108 cm. The cannon has a long handle behind the breech. The handle length is 49 cm.

Bortop 22 (ASM: 280)

The cannon is displayed at Assam State Museum in Guwahati. Its total length is 322 cm., and its barrel length is 200 cm. The trunnion length is 11.5 cm., and its diameter is 7 cm. The vent diameter is 2 cm. The muzzle's external diameter is 31 cm., and the bore diameter is 8.5 cm. The breech's external diameter is 32 cm. The distance between vent to muzzle is 196 cm., vent to breech base is 9 cm., trunnion to muzzle is 124 cm. and trunnion to breech base is 80 cm. The cannon has a long handle behind the breech. Its length is 107 cm. The handle also has a knob. The knob length is 12 cm, and its circumference is 48 cm.

Bortop 23 (Accession No. n/a)

The cannon is displayed at Assam State Museum in Guwahati. Its total length is 313 cm., and its barrel length is 255 cm. The trunnion length is 10 cm., and its diameter is 7 cm. The vent diameter is 2.5 cm. The muzzle's external diameter is 27 cm., and the bore diameter is 11 cm. The breech's external diameter is 27 cm. The distance between vent to muzzle is 258 cm., vent to breech base is 5 cm., trunnion to muzzle is 153 cm. and trunnion to breech base is 109 cm. The cannon has a broken handle behind the breech. The handle length is 37.5 cm.

Hilloi

Hilloi is a generic term used to describe a wide variety of Ahom light artillery or hand cannon. It comprises a barrel with a vent and a muzzle, a handle behind the breech base, and a stand attached to the trunnion. Specimens of *Hilloi* are preserved and displayed in the Assam State Museum in Guwahati, the District Museum in Jorhat, the District Museum in Dibrugarh, and the Ahom Tai Museum in Sivasagar.

Hilloi 1 (ASM: 278)

The *Hilloi* is displayed at Assam State Museum in Guwahati. It has an inscription, but it is not legible. Its total length is 112 cm., and its weight is 11 kg. Its barrel length is 70 cm. The *Hilloi* has trunnions, and attached to it is a stand. The trunnion length is 2 cm., and its diameter is 1.5 cm. The stand length is 25.5 cm. The vent diameter is 0.3 cm. The muzzle's external diameter is 5 cm., and the bore diameter is 2.5 cm. The breech's external diameter is 9 cm. The distance between vent to muzzle is 68.7 cm., vent to breech base is

2.5 cm., trunnion to muzzle is 39 cm. and trunnion to breech base is 33 cm. The *Hilloi* has a handle behind the breech. The handle length is 38.5 cm.

Hilloi 2 (ASM: 279)

The *Hilloi* is displayed at Assam State Museum in Guwahati. The *Hilloi* has an inscription in the Sanskrit language where the name of the Ahom queen Pramatheswari, with the date 1651 Saka, i.e., 1729 CE, is inscribed. Its total length is 88.6 cm., and its weight is 13.4 kg. Its barrel length is 80 cm. The *Hilloi* has trunnions, and attached to it is a stand. The trunnion length is 3 cm., and its diameter is 1.5 cm. The stand length is 28 cm. The vent diameter is 0.2 cm. The muzzle has a human face engraved in it. Two distinct round eyes with eyebrows and a prudent nose are visible. The muzzle's external diameter is 5.5 cm., and the bore diameter is 2.5 cm. The breech's external diameter is 8 cm. The distance between vent to muzzle is 79 cm., vent to breech base is 2.5 cm., trunnion to muzzle is 52.5 cm. and trunnion to breech base is 29.5 cm. The *Hilloi* has a broken handle behind the breech. The handle length is 5 cm.

Hilloi 3 (JDM/2019/652)

The *Hilloi* is displayed at the District Museum in Jorhat. Its total length is 102.5 cm., and its barrel length is 62.5 cm. The *Hilloi* has trunnions, and attached to it is a stand. The trunnion length is 2.5 cm., and its diameter is 2 cm. The vent diameter is 0.5 cm. The muzzle's external diameter is 5.3 cm., and the bore diameter is 2.6 cm. The breech's external diameter is 8 cm. The distance between vent to muzzle is 61 cm., vent to breech base is 2.5 cm., trunnion to muzzle is 36 cm. and trunnion to breech base is 26 cm. The *Hilloi* has a handle behind the breech. Its length is 36.5 cm. The handle also has a knob. The knob length is 2 cm, and its circumference is 13 cm.

Hilloi 4 (JDM/2022/651)

The *Hilloi* is displayed at the District Museum in Jorhat. The *Hilloi* has an inscription in which the name of Ahom monarch Gadadhar Simha, along with the weapon's name, i.e., *Ramchangi*, is inscribed. Its total length is 126.5 cm., and its weight is 15 kg. Its barrel length is 79 cm. The *Hilloi* has trunnions, and attached to it is a stand. The trunnion length is 2.5 cm., and its diameter is 1.5 cm. The stand length is 31.2 cm. The vent diameter is 1 cm. The muzzle's external diameter is 6 cm., and the bore diameter is 3 cm. The breech's external diameter is 10 cm. The distance between vent to muzzle is 77.5 cm., vent to breech base is 2.5 cm., trunnion to muzzle is 46 cm. and trunnion to breech base is 34 cm. The *Hilloi* has a handle behind the breech. Its length is 43.5 cm. The handle also has a knob. The knob length is 2 cm, and its circumference is 12 cm.

Hilloi 5 (DMD/294/2015/01)

The *Hilloi* is displayed at the District Museum in Dibrugarh. Its total length is 167 cm., and its barrel length is 109 cm. The *Hilloi* has trunnions, and attached to it is a stand. The trunnion length is 3 cm. and its diameter is 1.8 cm. The stand length is 44.5 cm. The vent diameter is 0.5 cm. The muzzle's external diameter is 8 cm., and the bore diameter is 2.5 cm. The breech's external diameter is 15 cm. The distance between the vent to the breech base is 3 cm. The trunnion to the muzzle is 65 cm. The trunnion to the breech base is 44 cm. The *Hilloi* has a handle behind the breech. Its length is 55 cm. The handle also has a knob. The knob length is 2 cm. and its diameter is 3.5 cm.

Hilloi 6 (DMD/199/94/01)

The *Hilloi* is displayed at the District Museum in Dibrugarh. Its total length is 74 cm., and its weight is 9.6 kg. Its barrel length is 68 cm. The trunnion length is 2.5 cm., and its diameter is 1.5 cm. The muzzle's external diameter is 5.4 cm. The breech's external diameter is 6.5 cm. The distance between the trunnion and the muzzle is 38 cm. The trunnion to the breech base is 31 cm.

Hilloi 7 (Chamber No. 7: 54)

The *Hilloi* is displayed at the Ahom Tai Museum in Sivasagar. Its total length is 122 cm., and its barrel length is 79.5 cm. The barrel has eleven rings. The *Hilloi* has trunnions, and attached to it is a stand. The trunnion length is 3 cm., and its diameter is 2 cm. The stand length is 29 cm. The vent diameter is 1.5 cm. The muzzle's external diameter is 8 cm., and the bore diameter is 3 cm. The breech's external diameter is 9 cm. The distance between vent to muzzle is 78 cm., vent to breech base is 2 cm., trunnion to muzzle is 51 cm. and trunnion to breech base is 30.5 cm. The *Hilloi* has a handle behind the breech. Its length is 41 cm.

Hilloi 8 (Chamber No. 7: 54)

The *Hilloi* is displayed at the Ahom Tai Museum in Sivasagar. Its total length is 101.5 cm., and its barrel length is 71 cm. The *Hilloi* has trunnions, and attached to it is a stand. The trunnion length is 2.5 cm., and its diameter is 2 cm. The stand length is 24 cm. The muzzle's external diameter is 5 cm., and the bore diameter is 2.5 cm. The distance between the trunnion and the muzzle is 39 cm. The trunnion to the breech base is 31.5 cm. The *Hilloi* has a handle behind the breech. Its length is 29 cm.

Hilloi 9 (Chamber No. 7: 54)

The *Hilloi* is displayed at the Ahom Tai Museum in Sivasagar. Its total length is 105 cm., and its barrel length is 71 cm. The *Hilloi* has trunnions, and attached to it is a stand. The trunnion length is 2 cm., and its diameter is 1.5 cm. The stand length is 24 cm. The muzzle's external diameter is 5 cm., and the bore diameter is 2.5 cm. The distance between the trunnion and the muzzle is 41 cm. The trunnion to the breech base is 32 cm. The *Hilloi* has a handle behind the breech. Its length is 30 cm.

Hilloi 10 (Chamber No. 7: 54)

The *Hilloi* is displayed at the Ahom Tai Museum in Sivasagar. It has an inscription in which the name of Ahom monarch Gadadhar Simha is inscribed. Its total length is 98.5 cm., and its barrel length is 93.5 cm. The trunnion length is 4 cm., and its diameter is 2.5 cm. The vent diameter is 1.5 cm. The muzzle's external diameter is 9 cm., and the bore diameter is 4 cm. The distance between vent to muzzle is 86 cm., vent to breech base is 3 cm., trunnion to muzzle is 55 cm., and trunnion to breech base is 36 cm. The *Hilloi* has two holding bars. One is 8.5 cm. long while the other is 9 cm. long.

Gulli

A round metal or stone ball launched from a *Bortop* or *Hilloi* is called a *Gulli*. The terminology of *Gulli* depends on its shape and size, and it is often synonymized with the names of nuts and fruits. For instance, *Maah Gulli, Bogori* (Indian jujube or *Ziziphus mauritiana*) *Gulli, Tokou Gulli, Tamul* (Areca nut or *Areca catechu*) *Gulli, Bel* (Wood apple or *Aegel marmelos*) *Gulli*, and *Lau* (Calabash or *Lagenaria siceraria*) *Gulli* (Buragohain 2022, p. 18). These were made of stone and are currently preserved and displayed in the Ahom Tai Museum in Sivasagar, the District Museum in Dibrugarh, the Assam State Museum in Guwahati, and the District Museum in Jorhat.

Ahom Tai Museum in Sivasagar (Chamber No. 7: 55)

The Ahom Tai Museum in Sivasagar preserves and displays ten *Gulli*. The circumference and weight of these are provided in the below table 1:

Table 1: Gulli from Ahom Tai Museum, Sivasagar

Sl. No.	Circumference of Gulli (in cm.)	Weight of Gulli (in kg.)
1.	38	2.1
2.	32.5	1.4
3.	32	1.5
4.	31	1.1
5.	27	0.8
6.	13.5	0.2
7.	13.5	0.2
8.	11.5	-
9.	11.5	-
10.	10.6	-

(*source*: author)

District Museum in Dibrugarh (DMD/275/14/01)

The District Museum in Dibrugarh preserves and displays five *Gulli*. The circumference and weight of these are provided in the below table 2:

Table 2: Gulli from District Museum, Dibrugarh

Sl. No.	Circumference of Gulli (in cm.)	Weight of Gulli (in kg.)
1.	25.1	0.6
2.	20.5	0.3
3.	19	0.2
4.	14	-
5.	12	-

(*source*: author)

Assam State Museum in Guwahati (Accession No. n/a)

The Assam State Museum in Guwahati preserves and displays twenty-eight _Gulli_. The circumference and weight of these are provided in the below table 3:

Table 3: Gulli from Assam State Museum, Guwahati

Sl. No.	Circumference of Gulli (in cm.)	Weight of Gulli (in kg.)
1.	28.5	0.9
2.	26.7	0.7
3.	25	0.6
4.	22.5	0.4
5.	21	0.4
6.	22	0.4
7.	22	0.4
8.	18	0.2
9.	18.5	0.2
10.	18	0.2
11.	17.5	0.2
12.	16.5	0.2
13.	14	-
14.	13	-
15.	13.5	-
16.	12.5	-
17.	12	-
18.	12	-
19.	11.5	-
20.	10	-

Sl. No.	Circumference of Gulli (in cm.)	Weight of Gulli (in kg.)
21.	10.5	-
22.	10.3	-
23.	9.5	-
24.	9	-
25.	9.5	-
26.	9.5	-
27.	9	-
28.	9	-

(*source*: author)

District Museum in Jorhat (Accession No. JDM/2019/183-JDM/2019/189)

The District Museum in Jorhat preserves and displays seven *Gulli*. The circumference and weight of these are provided in the below table 4:

Table 4: Gulli from District Museum, Jorhat

Sl. No.	Circumference of Gulli (in cm.)	Weight of Gulli(in kg.)
1.	26	0.6
2.	21.5	0.4
3.	22.5	0.5
4.	20.5	0.4
5.	20.5	0.4
6.	19.5	0.3
7.	18	0.3

(*source*: author)

Bow and Arrow

There is ambiguity among scholars regarding the types of bows or *Dhenu* used by the Ahom. Both Barpujari (1994) and Gogoi (2006) maintain that the Ahom used three types of bows: *Bar-dhenu, Chutiya-dhenu,* and *Karfai-dhenu.* However, Gogoi (2017) and Buragohain (2022) extend the list to sixteen bows, including *Baagh-dhenu, Batolugutir-dhenu, Beehkar-dhenu, Borahi-dhenu, Choonga-dhenu, Deu-dhenu, Haat-dhenu, Indra-dhenu, Jati-dhenu, Juikar-dhenu, Miri-dhenu, Moran-dhenu, Naga-dhenu, Phank-dhenu, Tai-dhenu,* and *Teelikar-dhenu.* Yet not all of these were of Ahom origin. For instance, the Ahom learned the utility of *Bar-dhenu* and *Chutiya-dhenu* after the annexation of the Bhuyan domain and Chutiya kingdom. Similarly, they learned to use *Miri-dhenu* from the Miri, *Naga-dhenu* from the Naga, and *Moran-dhenu* from the Moran.

Regarding the types of arrows or *Kar*, the Ahom used bamboo arrows with or without iron heads. Baishya (2009) and Gogoi (2017) mention the name of Ahom used arrows. These were *Bihyukta-kar, Karfaidhenu-kar, Khaja-kar, Lohayukta-kar, Palengpatia-kar, Singimuri-kar,* and *Topa-kar.* Some arrows also had poison, such as *Singimuri-kar* (Baishya 2009, p. 305). However, tangible Ahom bow and arrow specimens do not exist in the museums across Assam. Perhaps as these were made of perishable objects, such as wood or bamboo, these could not bear the test of time.

Chapter 05

Defensive Weapon

A wielder uses a defensive weapon, which may or may not be handheld, to defend themselves from an opponent's attack. Some examples of defensive armaments are shields, armor, helmets, etc. Though such weapons are not designed for offensive purposes, they could be, if the user deems them, can be used to inflict bodily harm.

Defensive Weapon

The Ahom used various defensive weapons, including shields like *Baru*, *Dhal*, and *Phar*. *Dhal* again had different varieties, such as *Buka-dhal*, *Deu-dhal*, *Dhigol-dhal*, *Gaa-dhal*, *Haat-dhal*, *Pakhi-dhal*, and *Suri-dhal* (Buragohain 2022, p. 18). According to Gogoi (2006), *Baru* and *Dhal* were revolving shields. Yet the difference among *Baru*, *Dhal*, and *Phar* remains in the size and construction material. While *Dhal* was made of buffalo hide or rhinoceros skin, *Baru* and *Phar* were made of bamboo and cane (Gogoi 2017, p. 49). Regarding size, *Baru* was larger than *Dhal*, and *Phar* was larger than *Baru* as it covered the entire body (Barpujari 1994, p. 72; Gogoi 2006, p. 97).

Apart from the shields, the Ahom also used a thick skin jacket called *Gati* and a helmet called *Takaya* for defensive purposes (Gogoi 2006, p. 97; Baishya 2009, p. 305). Gogoi (2017) also mentions other defensive weapons that do not directly protect the soldier's body but counter or block the enemy's advance in battle. This type of Ahom defensive weapon included *Chak*, *Jong*, *Magha*, and *Singari*. *Chak*, *Jong*, and *Magha* were different varieties of bamboo pike with sharp heads. These were inserted on the ground to block the enemy's path. On the other hand, *Singari* had small iron spikes scattered on the pathway.

Dhal

Although the literature mentions different types of Ahom shield, i.e., *Baru*, *Dhal*, and *Phar*, the museums across Assam preserve and display only *Dhal*. The specimens of *Dhal* are in the Assam State Museum in Guwahati, the District Museum in Dibrugarh, and the Ahom Tai Museum in Sivasagar. The table below provides the dimension of the *Dhal*:

Table 5: Dhal from Museum across Assam

Sl. No.	Museum	Shape	Diameter (cm.)	Weight (kg.)
1.	Assam State Museum, Guwahati	Circular	67	-
2.	Assam State Museum, Guwahati	Circular	41	-
3.	District Museum, Dibrugarh	Circular	47	0.9
4.	Ahom Tai Museum, Sivasagar	Circular	61.5	-

(*source*: author)

Chapter 06

Smelters and Blacksmiths

The Ahom chronicles[33] narrate a mythical story regarding the utility of *Lik* (iron) by the Ahom divinity named Khunlung and Khunlai. According to the story, after greeting Lengdon and other deities, the two princes, wearing shining coats and golden caps, left the heavenly palace for *Mongri* (a habitable middle country). On their way, they were welcomed by celestial nymphs, and after bidding farewell to everyone, they took hold of the *Lik-Khang* (iron ladder) and proceeded downwards with the motion of the wind. Soon, they arrived in *Mongri*, placed the golden throne there, raised the royal umbrella, and sat on the throne.

So, how far is the story true? That remains ambiguous. Yet what is unambiguous is that the Ahom knew the utilization of iron before their advent in the Brahmaputra Valley. For instance, the *Satsari Assam Buranji* (Bhuyan 1960) and the *Assam Buranji* (Bhuyan 1945) mention that the Ahom carried iron-forged weapons, such as *Hengdang, Jathi,* etc., on their journey to the valley. Then, another Tai chronicle (Phukan *et al.* 1998) mentions that the Ahom under Sukapha started manufacturing weapons in large quantities for battles after crossing the *Nam-Jin* (Buri-Dihing) River. So, it is evident that the Ahom were familiar with forging. However, did they know the mining and smelting of iron ore?

They did, as evidenced by Baishya's (2009) account, which notes that Sukapha drank water from various rivers and discovered that the water of the Dikhow River was heavier than other rivers. Therefore, he inquired and found that Tiru Hill had iron ore deposits and, from there, ascended a small stream called Tiru, which drained its water in the Dikhow River, making its water heavy. Sukapha then established a smelting workshop in the Tiru Hill area. Thus, from these references, it is argued that the Ahom, before they arrived in the Brahmaputra Valley, were accustomed to the knowledge of forging weapons and mining and smelting iron ore.

However, the question remains––what were the Ahom sources of iron ore? What was the Ahom mining, smelting, and forging technology like? Did they resort to the iron ore sources in their kingdom, or was there any other source? If there was any other source, what was it? And why were they resorting to other sources? In this chapter, an attempt is made to answer these questions.

Indigenous Source

Hannay (1856) considers the whole southern frontier adjoining the Naga Hills, south of the present-day Dibrugarh, Sivasagar, and Golaghat districts, a region roughly between Jaipur and Doyang River, to be rich in iron ore (Figure 1). Hannay (1856) notes that the Ahom monarchy built large establishments for smelting iron ores in this region. Hunter (1879) further substantiates Hannay's account and provides evidence of iron ore in Sivasagar, Jaipur, and Barhat. Apart from these regions, there were some localities where iron ore deposition and associated activities, such as mining and smelting, were more prominent. The first region was Tirugaon Hill and Hattigarh. This area was rich in iron ore deposits, and Hannay (1856) considered the iron ore of this region to be "the best, both as to the quality and quantity of the ores." Second, the region was of Bossa and Doyang. Here, iron ore was obtained from the ferruginous clay (Pemberton 1835), and according to Hamilton (1940), the iron ore mine of Doyang used to supply "the whole country (i.e., Ahom kingdom) with abundance." The third region was the bank of the Suffrai River. Robinson (1841) observed the remains of furnaces in the nearby areas of Jaipur, Barhat, and the Suffrai River banks.

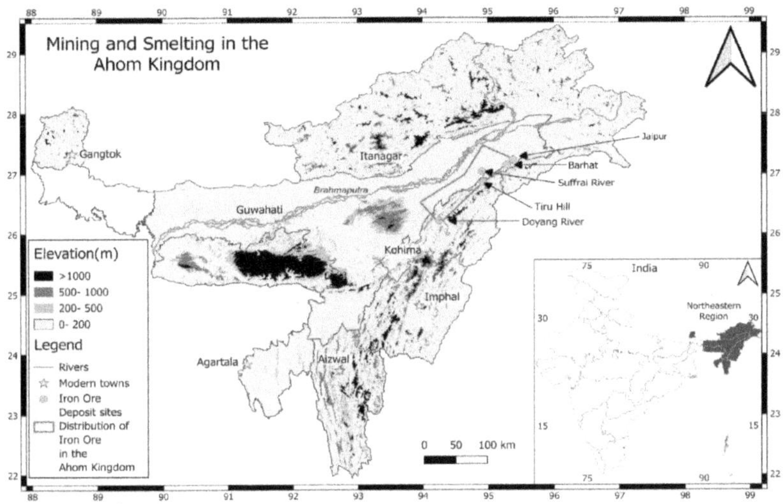

Figure 1: Areas Associated with Mining and Smelting in the Ahom Kingdom (*source*: **author**)

Mining and Smelting

The availability of iron ore in the Ahom kingdom led to the development of the iron industry in the Brahmaputra Valley (Purkayastha 2007). But who was engaged with mining, smelting, and later forging? And what was their technology like? According to Borboruah (1981), two separate guilds[34] of artisans one for mining and smelting of iron ore, called *Losalia* or *Tiruwal,* and the other for blacksmithing work, called *Kamar*--were engaged with the iron industry during the Ahom rule. The origin of the smelter is associated with Sukapha himself, who initiated mining and smelting by establishing workshops and villages of iron smelters in Tiru Hill. For supervision, officers such as *Tiruwal Phu-Kin-Mong* (Rajkhowa) and *Tirukakati* (officer maintaining accounts) were appointed (Baishya 2009, pp. 300-301). Regarding the ethnic background of smelters, Purkayastha (2007) argues that they were comprised of Dimasa and Ahom ethnic groups. Moreover, she also postulates that smelters of the Brahmaputra Valley could have, in all possibility, maintained technological exchanges with the Kunung ethnic group, who, according to Robinson (1841), produced the "best iron." The Kunung people inhabited the Barkhampti area in Burma (now Myanmar).

Hannay (1856) describes the mining and smelting process of the smelter. At Bossa Doyang, he mentions that iron ore was obtained from ferruginous sand, deposited in a separate bed, and found at depths of ten, twelve, fifteen, and sixteen cubits under the surface. According to Hannay (1856), the mining process starts with finding beds containing iron ore, and the work takes about four to five days. Once the bed was located, six men were employed. Two of them used to dig out the lumps containing the oxide, the third took those and placed them at the entrance into the pit's pathway, the fifth took those lumps outside, and the sixth shaped those into a large rectangular heap. The dimension of the heap was about twelve cubits in length, seven cubits in breadth, and three to four cubits in height (Hannay 1856). Hence, six men working ten days collected one thousand maunds of iron ore-bearing clay in a heap. Once mined, the heap was divided into seven shares, which were equally distributed among themselves and their landlord. After that, the smelters washed the ore, which took ten to twelve days.

The ore's lumps are thrown in a large water pit where the smelters stamp the lump with their feet. Thus, iron ore was separated from the lumps. After washing and collecting iron ore, the smelting process starts by constructing a furnace. Hannay (1856) mentions that smelting was supervised by an *Ojha* (head smelter) who was also required to draw out the melted lump of pig iron from every fifteen seers of iron ore. In addition to the *Ojha*, there were two other *Palee* (assistants). One assistant was entrusted with blowing the bellow while another brought iron ore and charcoal, which was thrown into the furnace. Thus, working daily, thirteen pieces of pig iron were extracted by smelting. One of the necessary items required during the smelting process is *Hadora*, an open-hearth furnace with a bowl-shaped pit on the ground. Its circumference was covered with hardened clay. *Bhatti* or *Hatina*, a bellow made of goatskin and *angar*, i.e., hardened wood, was used for combustion (Baishya 2009, p. 302).

Forging

The organization of blacksmiths as a guild is associated with the annexation of the Chutiya kingdom in 1523 CE by Suhungmung (Purkayastha 2007). According to the *Satsari Assam Buranji* (Bhuyan 1960), the annexation led to the migration of Chutiya artisans,[35] including a blacksmith, into the Ahom kingdom. The blacksmiths who were settled in the vicinity of Bossa established many smithy workshops and were required to produce and supply weapons, such as swords, cannons, etc., to the royal storehouse (Sarma 1950, pp. 275-276; Borboruah 1981, p. 466). However, in the western part of the Ahom kingdom, the blacksmith guild that supplied weapons belonged to the Kolita and Koch groups. They made spears, light artillery, sacrificial choppers, etc. (Hamilton 1940, p. 62). Hence, Purkayastha (2007) argues that the social organization of the blacksmith guild in the Ahom kingdom varied according to region. The officers such as *Ru-Pak* (Saikia) and *Ru-Ring* (Hazarika) supervised the blacksmith guild (Hannay 1856).

The blacksmith guild used pig iron to forge various kinds of weapons. The lumps of pig iron, according to Hannay (1856), "were sold for two, three, or four annas a piece, according to quantity and quality of pure malleable iron." The blacksmith established their forging workshop in many places. Nath (1948) has noted the location of forging centers. These were--Messa (26° 29' 06.0" N. lat. and 92° 56' 46.7" E. long.), Messamara (26° 39' 47.9" N. lat. and 93° 55' 26.8" E. long.), Dergaon (26° 41' 48.8" N. lat. and 93° 59' 07.1" E. long.), Kamarbandha (26° 31' 45.6" N. lat. and 94° 03' 13.4" E. long.), Kamargaon (26° 38' 37.0" N. lat. and 93° 46' 53.8" E. long.), Denkial (26° 36' 09.7" N. lat. and 93° 59' 07.1" E. long.) and Dadhara (26° 41' 08.9" N. lat. and 93° 55' 55.6" E. long.).

The forging of an edged weapon starts as a blacksmith places a metal in the forge with heated charcoal and uses the bellow to blow air into it. The bellow was made of goatskin and fixed with two bamboo pieces at the rear end. More charcoal was added if necessary. Thus, heating continues until the metal reaches a temperature where it can be moved to a *Niyari* (anvil) for hammering. Baishya (2009) mentions that there are four types of anvils. These were *Bor-niyari* (or large anvils used for hammering large metal pieces), *Belmuri* (or medium-sized anvil whose base was pointed and fixed on a wooden piece), *Dheka* (another medium-sized anvil with a sharp point on both ends), and *Chatuli* (a small sized anvil).

The heated metal was removed from the forge using a *Sarah* or tong. Baishya (2009) mentions that the blacksmith used six types of tongs to lift, grip, and move the heated metal. These were *Pat-sarah* (its front end was flat), *Akora-sarah* (its front end was twisted), *Chenidhara-sarah* (used to hold *Cheni* or cutter), *Gall-sarah* (its front end was twisted towards the back), *Beji-sarah* (a small tong used to pick tiny objects), and *Pon-sarah* (forceps). Once removed, the blacksmith kept the heated metal in the anvil and used a cutter to remove impurities. Then, he pounded the metal with *Haturi* (hammer) to derive the required shape of the weapon. If the metal got cold, it was again placed in the forge for heating. Repeated heating and hammering continued until the desired shape was acquired.

Baishya (2009) mentions that the blacksmith used a variety of hammers. These were *Bor-haturi* (large hammer), *Topalagoch* (medium-sized hammer), and *Mathani* (small hammer used for engraving and gilding). After acquiring the desired shape of the weapon, the blacksmith profiled it to remove the hammer marks and other impurities. Then, it was reheated for quenching on a *Noara* (water pot). After this, the blacksmith checked if the metal was hardened or not. If it remained soft, then the metal was reheated for quenching. The last step was the construction of the handle, using animal bone, horn, or wood. The handle was attached to the blade by either heating the tang and inserting it into the handle or pinning it to the tang using rivets (pin).

However, considering the forging of a cannon, Buragohain (2022) argues that these were made in separate segments and later joined together to produce the desired shape. He further contends that copper was also used for manufacturing cannon apart from iron. Hannay's (1856) report lists forging workshops in the Ahom kingdom and their total output (Table 6).

Table 6: Production of Firearms in the Ahom Kingdom

Sl. No.	Firearm	Blacksmith workshops	Firearms manufactured per month
1.	Saru-hatnalia Hilloi	1	4
2.	Ramchangi Hilloi	1	2
3.	Pohulguri Hilloi	1	2
4.	Gathia Hilloi	1	1

Sl. No.	Firearm	Blacksmith workshops	Firearms manufactured per month
5.	Mithaholong Bortop	1	1
6.	Baghmura Bortop	1	1
7.	Tubuki Bortop	4	1
8.	Hatimuria Bortop	20	1
9.	Biagom Bortop	1	1

(*source*: Hannay 1856, p. 335; Gogoi 2006, p. 100; Purkayastha 2007, p. 156)

Trading Source

Although Ahom had many iron ore deposits in their kingdom, they still resorted to trade to procure pig iron from different regions. One of these regions was Mikir Hills, inhabited by the Mikir ethnic group who, along with various other articles, traded in iron with the Ahom (Phukan 1973, pp. 252-253). To facilitate trade between the Ahom and the Mikir, the Ahom monarchy established several *hat* (markets). For example, Susengpha set a market at Phulaguri on the bank of Kalang River; similarly, during the reign of Surampha, another market was set up at Roha (Bhuyan 1937, p. 17; Bhuyan 1932, p. 104). Another market located at Mikirhat was established on the left bank of the Kalang River. However, it was not just Mikir who traded pig iron with the Ahom. On the contrary, the Khasi and the Garo of the Khasi-Jaintia Hills and the Kunung ethnic group of the Bar Khamti region in Burma also traded in pig iron with the Ahom (Robinson 1841, p. 35; Borboruah 1981, p. 466; M'Cosh 1837, p. 58;

Leach 1954, p. 251). Nevertheless, Khasi held the lion's share of the pig iron trade.

After smelting iron ore, the Khasi bartered the pig iron in the plain regions (Cracroft 1832). Mills (1853) notes that Khasi kept very little of the smelted iron for themselves; instead, a significant portion was exported to Assam and Sylhet (now in the People's Republic of Bangladesh). To provide an extent of pig iron export from the Khasi Hill, Allen, in 1858, writes, "The average quantity of iron exported every year from the hills is probably 50,000 maunds." Allen (1858) also points out that the Khasi kept a tiny portion of pig iron for themselves, with which they forged tools, such as chopper, hoe, spear, etc., while the greater bulk was sold in circular lumps. However, the Khasi kept the best pig iron to themselves, which was shaped into flat bars called *Petee*. It was sold from one rupee to ten annas to one rupee twelve annas per maund. In contrast, the lump iron, *Berra*, had an average price of one rupee four annas to one rupee six annas per maund.

For trading, markets were essential, and every Khasi village had a market in its vicinity (Choudhury 1978, p. 68). The exchange was conducted through well-established trade routes through the hills via settlements, such as Nartiang, Jowai, and Jaintiapur on the Jaintia side and Nongkseh and Sorah on the Khasi side. Lish's (1838) account can be enumerated to highlight the trade between Khasi and the inhabitants of the Brahmaputra Valley. He mentioned that considerable intercourse was carried between the Khasi and the Assamese, from whom they got cloths of various kinds, such as *Mooga* and different colored silks, which were in high demand among the Khasi. Likewise, the Khasi supplied limestone to the Assamese, which was bountiful in the hills and a significant profit source for the Khasi. However, Khasi's greatest profit was derived from iron works.

The medium of exchange of articles,[36] including pig iron, produced in Khasi-Jaintia Hills, was barter. The Khasi-Ahom exchange of articles occurred at frontier markets, such as Ranihat, located in the territory of Raniraja, a tributary of the Ahom; Sonapur, in the region of Dimaruaraja; Palasbari; and Gohainhat (Phukan 1973, p. 151; Borboruah 1981, p. 466). The Ahom exchanged the Khasi articles, including pig iron with mustard, cloth, silk, rice, salt, tobacco, goat, etc. (Pemberton 1835, p. 215; Robinson 1841, p. 408; Choudhury 1978, p. 69; Borboruah 1981, p. 466). On bartering, Lish (1838) describes that the Khasi had the habit of bartering their hill produce with those living in the plains. They sold oranges, honey, pig iron, bee's wax, ivory, rubber, etc., in exchange for rice, fish, salt, and spices. Now, the question is--why were the Ahom importing pig iron from the Khasi? There are two particular reasons:

First, as Purkayastha (2007) points out, the quantity of iron smelted by the Ahom smelters proved insufficient to fulfill the demand of blacksmiths engaged in forging weapons. Yet what caused this insufficiency in the first place? Was there a shortage of iron ore, or was there any technological lagging in the smelting procedure that had resulted in pig iron's low productivity? According to Purkayastha (2007), the Ahom smelters had some technical deficiencies in smelting compared to their Khasi counterpart. For example, the smelters in the Ahom kingdom used an open-air furnace while the smelters of Khasi Hills used an indoor furnace, i.e., they had a smelting house (Borboruah 1981, p. 466). It was a minor variation but significantly impacted the production of pig iron. To elicit how this variation affected, Purkayastha (2007) writes, "The use of open-air furnaces proves that the smelters were engaged in smelting iron only at a particular period in a year. The lack of smelting houses further testifies to their less productive technology than the Khasi smelters. Therefore, the supply was insufficient to the demand, and they had to depend on the Khasi smelters for crude iron."

The second reason was the quality of the Khasi pig iron, which led the Ahom monarchy to import it in large quantities. In the *Memoirs of the Geological Survey of India,* there is a reference to the Khasi pig iron's superior quality. Thomas Oldham (1859) remarks, "The quality of the Khasi iron is excellent for all such purposes as Swedish iron is now used for." He says, "It (Khasi iron) would also form steel or *wootz* of excellent quality." Similarly, Allen (1858) notes the quality and availability of Khasi pig iron as he writes, "The ore is said to be of the best quality and most abundant in the Khyrim country, and the purest and most superior sort is found at Nungkreem and Nogundree in that district." Therefore, as it turns out, and to quote Hannay (1856), "The Khasi iron from its soft and malleable nature was considered the best for the manufacture of nails, firearms of small size, and the inner tubes of the large cannons; the iron of the Upper Assam ores being found best adapted for swords, axes, knives, shovels, and hoes, etc."

Tributary Source

Indigenous mining, smelting, and trading with neighboring regions were not the only modes of acquiring pig iron by the Ahom; instead, there was another source--tribute. Annual tribute, which was in kind, formed a significant source of income for the Ahom. Since their rule in the 13th century CE, the Ahom received annual tribute from tributary chiefs, frontier ethnic groups, and provincial governors (Phukan 1973, p. 88). Accordingly, the eastern provinces of Khamjang, Aiton, and Tipam were the Ahom tributaries and the Naga of Namchang, Banchang, Jabaka, and Tabloong. Similarly, the ethnic groups of the hill, such as the Miri, Mishimi, Mikir, and Bhutia, also paid tribute, so did the frontier Rajas of Rani, Dimarua, Ghiladhari, Beltola, Dihing, Kharangi, Sat-rajas, Panch-rajas, Bebejia, Mayang, Panbari, Chundoria, and Dooria. Darrang Raja and the Dimasa monarch, too, paid tribute (Phukan 1973, p. 88-92).

Among the ethnic groups and kingdoms, the Dimasa kingdom is significant, as their tribute article included pig iron, horses, cloth, and *Nakoi-da* (Bhuyan 1945). But how did the Dimasa become an Ahom tributary? Refer to Chapter 3, where an elaborate discussion is provided on the Ahom-Dimasa relation, the enforcement of "established and preserved" status to the Dimasa by the Ahom, and the subsequent payment of annual tribute in kind. Thus, from the discussion, it is evident that the Ahom had three ways of procuring pig iron: first, through indigenous mining and smelting in areas such as Bossa and Doyang, Hattigarh, Tiru Hill, and Suffrai River bank. Second, through trade with neighboring ethnic groups, such as the Khasi, and third, through tribute from the Dimasa kingdom. The blacksmith guild then used the collective quantity to forge weapons of various kinds.

Chapter 07

Findings

As the book title suggests, it attempts to understand an unknown aspect of Ahom's tangible culture, i.e., weapons. Thus, each chapter explores a different type of Ahom weapon, ranging from sword to firearm to shield. In this process, the primary objective was to document and describe the weapons held in various institutions across Assam. So forth, a total of one hundred and twenty-seven weapons–ten *Jathi*, four *Barsha*, one *Khapor*, two *Hengdang*, seven swords, nine *Nakoi-da*, one *Shikara-da*, twenty-five *Bortop*, thirteen *Hilloi*, fifty-one *Gulli*, and four *Dhal*, preserved and displayed in Assam State Museum in Guwahati, Cottage Industries Museum in Guwahati, Ahom Tai Museum in Sivasagar, Talatalghar in Sivasagar District Museum in Jorhat, District Museum in Mangaldoi, District Museum in Tezpur, and District Museum in Dibrugarh are described. The collected information is then corroborated with the chronicle and a synthesis, thus formed, helped fill the knowledge gap.

Other issues associated with Ahom weapons are also discussed besides the documentation of weapons. For example, the issue over classifying Ahom weapons. In the second chapter, Ahom weapons were grouped into melee, ranged, and defensive weapons. However, in the same chapter, it is also suggested that the grouping of weapons changes as per its function. For example, melee weapons such as a dagger or an axe can be used as a ranged weapon if thrown from hand. Hence, the very nature of dividing weapons is subjected to alteration, and not just based on function but also considering other factors; as such, Ahom weapons can also be approached with a novel classification:

- Weapons of Ahom origin–this would include the weapons brought by the Ahom from their native land, *Mongmao*. Evidence of such edged weapons is corroborated in the *Assam Buranji* (Bhuyan 1945) and the *Satsari Assam Buranji* (Bhuyan 1960). According to these chronicles, the Ahom came to the Brahmaputra Valley with weapons, such as *Hengdang, Jathi, Dhenu,* etc. After the establishment of the Ahom kingdom, these weapons were produced in large quantities (Phukan *et al.* 1998, p. 24)

- Weapons acquired as a *Choi* (tribute)–this would include weapons supplied to the Ahom as tribute by the subjugated ethnic groups and kingdoms. For example, the chronicle states that Khamjang, Aitan, and Tipam used to pay tribute to the Ahom monarchs, including weapons such as *Nara-da* (Phukan 1973, p. 88). Similarly, the Miri paid tributes in *Shikara-da*, as did the Dimasa in *Nakoi-da* (Phukan 1973, pp. 89-90). In addition, the subjugated Naga of Banchang, Jabaka, Namchang, etc., also supplied weapons, such as *Naga-jathi* (Phukan 1973, p. 89)

- Weapons collected as war booty–the Ahom used to collect war booty in battles. For instance, during Suhungmung's campaign against the Chutiya kingdom in 1523 CE and also against the Dimasa kingdom in 1531 CE, weapons were collected in large quantities. Moreover, during the same monarch's reign, Bengal generals Bit Manik and Turbak Khan invaded the Ahom Kingdom in 1527 CE and 1532 CE. In these battles, too, the Ahom captured war booty. Moreover, in the 17th century CE, the Ahom were engaged in war against the Mughal. During the Ahom-Mughal War, the Ahom also collected war booty

This type of classification has certain advantages. For instance, it does not limit the Ahom weapon to merely a sword, spear, or firearm; instead, it expands the study's scope. In other words, such a classification helps to understand the Ahom interaction with neighboring ethnic groups and kingdoms with whom weapons were exchanged as tribute or war booty and technology. Moreover, the weapons acquired as tribute or war booty also formed the bulk of Ahom weapons as they later used them in battles (Gogoi 2017, p. 47). Therefore, considering the advantages, the Ahom weapon is classified differently.

Another aspect of the work is to highlight the ways in which the Ahom procured iron ore and pig iron for manufacturing weapon. There were three ways. First, through indigenous mining and smelting. For this purpose, the Ahom created a smelter's guild. The guild mined iron ore from Tirugaon Hill, Hattigarh, the area between Bossa and Doyang, and from Suffrai River bank. Once mined, the iron ore was smelted in a furnace. The blacksmith then used the pig iron to forge weapons of various types. Second way of obtaining pig iron was by trade with neighbouring ethnic groups of which the Khasi had the major share. The Khasis bartered pig iron in exchange for mustard, cloth, silk, rice, salt, tobacco, etc. The trading activity mainly occurred in markets at Ranihat, Gohainhat, Sonapur, Palasbari, etc. Third way of obtaining pig iron was by tribute from the Dimasa kingdom, who offered pig iron, among other articles. Once obtained, the blacksmith used the pig iron to forge weapons.

Then, there is the issue of firearm usage by the Ahom. According to the conventional view, such as Wade (1800) and Gait (1905), the Turko-Afghan generals from Bengal introduced a firearm to the Ahom in 1527 CE or 1532 CE. However, their proposition cannot be supported because the Chutiya were using firearms before these dates. As such, after the Ahom-Chutiya war in 1523 CE, Ahom acquired *Mithaholong* cannon and *Hilloi* from the Chutiya. Moreover, after the war, Ahom monarch Suhungmung relocated many Chutiya blacksmiths from the Sadiya region and settled them in the Ahom kingdom. These blacksmiths were required to produce various war armaments, including firearms, for the Ahom monarchy.

Hence, it is reasonable to argue that by the early 1520, the Ahom owned firearms, while the Chutiya could possess them from a much earlier date. Similarly, based on the evidence from the *Kachari Buranji* (Bhuyan 1936), it is evident that the Dimasa kingdom also possessed firearms from the early 15th century CE. As such, they used them in combat against the Ahom in 1473 CE. This assertion is also supported by a foreign account. For instance, Jean-Baptiste Tavernier, a French merchant, and traveler who visited India in the 17th century CE, writes:

> It is believed that this people in ancient times first discovered gunpowder and guns, which passed from Assam to Pegu to China; this is the reason why the discovery is generally ascribed to the Chinese. Mir Jumla brought back from this war numerous iron guns, and the gunpowder made in that country is excellent. Its grain is not long as in the kingdom of Bhutan, but is round and small like ours, and is much more effective than the other powder...He (the Ahom monarch) had many guns, and an abundance of fireworks, somewhat like our grenades, which are fixed at the end of a stick as long as a short pike...and carry more than 500 paces.[37]

Thus, the chronicle and foreign account imply two things. First, the Ahom knew the utility of firearms and gunpowder before Turbak's invasion in 1532 CE; and second, they had their way of manufacturing firearms and gunpowder, which they could have learned from their interaction with neighboring kingdoms, such as Chutiya and Dimasa. However, there remains a question--how did the Chutiya and Dimasa kingdoms come to possess firearms and gunpowder? There is substantial evidence to support that gunpowder for the explosion was developed in China by 1230 CE, and from there, it spread to all directions through maritime and overland routes (Goodrich and Chia-sheng 1946, pp. 114-123; Ling 1947, pp. 160-178; Laichen 2003, pp. 495-517). Could it be that the Chutiya and Dimasa learned the gunpowder recipe and firearm technology from their overland interaction with China?

Tavernier's account also mentions gunpowder and "gun" being first used in Assam and then passed to Pegu and later China. Whether Tavernier's account is valid is uncertain. However, from his account, what is certain is that the kingdoms of Brahmaputra Valley had close interaction with China in matters of gunpowder technology from an early stage (Khan 1994, pp. 194-200). It would be too early to derive any conclusion, but it does open new avenues for research.

Another issue is dealt with in the book in terms of firearms. The problem is regarding Ahom's usage of matchlock. Gait (1905), in his book *A History of Assam,* mentions that Ahom firearms include "cannon" and "matchlock". Though there is material and literary evidence to prove that the Ahom were indeed using cannons from the 16th century CE and flint guns from the late 18th century CE, there is no single evidence to testify to Gait's account that they had matchlock guns. Instead, they had a hand cannon of varied shape and size, which Gait has mistaken as a matchlock gun.

Then there are the works of Barpujari (1994) and Gogoi (2006), who repeated Gait's mistake of identifying *Hilloi* with a matchlock, adding more to the confusion. Their work identifies eleven types of *Hilloi,* including *Ramchangi.* However, in chapter four of the book, a specimen of *Ramchangi* (e.g., *Hilloi* 4) is described, and from the description, it is clear that it is not a matchlock gun. Instead, it is a hand cannon. Thus, it is argued that Barpujari (1994) and Gogoi (2006) made a doubtful identification due to the lack of material evidence. However, it led to the question of the nature of *Hilloi*, i.e., if it is not a matchlock, what is it? We have suggested that *Hilloi* is a generic term that describes a wide variety of Ahom light artillery, comprising a barrel with a vent and a muzzle, a handle behind the breech base, and a stand attached to the trunnion.

Notes

1   The Brahmaputra River is known by many names. In the *Mahabharata*, Brahmaputra River is noted as *Moyal Tirtha* whereas in the *Kalika Purana*, *Skanda Purana* and *Bhagavat Purana* it is referred as the 'son of Brahma'. However, the *Matsya Purana* denotes the river *Lauhitya Sarovara*. The Ahom named it as *Nam-Ti-Lao* ('nam' = water + 'ti' = a place + 'lao' = to infatuate, meaning a river from a beautiful place). The river among other Tai groups, is known as *Nam-Dao-Phi* ('nam' = water + 'dao' = a star + 'phi' = a god, meaning a river of star-god). For further detail on the terminology, refer to A.C. Sharma, The Brahmaputra Through the Ages in *Pragjyotisapura Through Ages*, Guwahati, 1996, pp. 62-64; R.S.G. Borua, *Ahom-Assamese-English-Dictionary*, Calcutta, 1920, pp. 40-41; N. Gogoi, Ahom Warfare: Lessons Drawn from the Ahom Buranji, *Tai Culture Interdisciplinary Tai Studies Series*, 21, pp. 57-63.

2   The term *Buranji* ('bu' = ignorant persons + 'ran' = teach + 'ji' = store) means a store that teaches the ignorant. These are chronicles written in Tai Language, and deals with the reign of Ahom monarchs. Most of the chronicles are translated into Assamese and English Language and are kept in the Department of Historical and Antiquarian Studies (DHAS) in Guwahati, Assam.

3   *Mongmao* was a Tai province in southwestern Yunnan in China until its abolition in 1952 CE. Currently, this region in China is known as Ruili (24° 00' 46.1" N. lat. and 97° 51' 06.8" E. long.), and it is in Dehong Dai-Singpho Autonomous Prefecture.

4   Khamjang River comes out of Nongyang Lake and meets the Chindwin River, see B.K. Gohain, *Origin of the Tai and Chao Lung Hsukapha*, New Delhi, 1999, p. 76.

5   Nongyang Lake (27° 13' 09.0" N. lat. and 96° 08' 37.9" E. long.) is situated on the other side of the Khamjang River, along the current Indo-Myanmar border; see B.K. Gohain, *Origin of the Tai and Chao Lung Hsukapha*, New Delhi, 1999, p. 75.

6   *Mong-Dun-Sun-Kham* ('*mong*' = province + '*dun*' = full + '*sun*' = garden + '*kham*' = gold) means a country full of golden garden.

7   Habung ('*ha*' = land + '*bung*' = low) would comprise the area between Dihing and Lohit River, see B.K. Gohain, *Origin of the Tai and Chao Lung Hsukapha*, New Delhi, 1999, p. 77.

8   For a detail description on the Ahom-Chutiya war, refer to G.C. Barua, *Ahom Buranji*, Gauhati, 1930, pp. 54-58; S.K. Bhuyan, *Assam Buranji*, Gauhati, 1945, pp. 8-11; S.K. Bhuyan, *Deodhai Assam Buranji*, Gauhati, 1932, pp. 13-15; S.K. Bhuyan, *Satsari Assam Buranji*, Gauhati, 1960, pp. 56-59.

9   Birnarayan, according to, S.K. Bhuyan, *Satsari Assam Buranji*, Gauhati, 1960, p. 56.

10   For a detail description on the Ahom-Dimasa war, refer to G.C. Barua, *Ahom Buranji*, Gauhati, 1930, pp. 58-66; S.K. Bhuyan, *Assam Buranji*, Gauhati, 1945, pp. 11-19; S.K. Bhuyan, *Deodhai Assam Buranji*, Gauhati, 1932, pp. 17-28; S.K. Bhuyan, *Satsari Assam Buranji*, Gauhati, 1960, pp. 62-66.

11   See, H. Goswami, *Purani Assam Buranji*, Gauhati, 1922, p. 63; S.K. Bhuyan, *Kamrupar Buranji*, Guwahati, 1930, p. 20; S.K. Bhuyan, *Satsari Assam Buranji*, Gauhati, 1960, p. 27.

12   The Mughal officials were Raja Jagdeo, Gandharva Rai, Raja Rai, Kala Raja, Hara Pratap Singh, Indramani, Narasingha Rai, Bhagwan Rai and Karamchand, see, S.K. Bhuyan, *Kamrupar Buranji*, Gauhati, 1930, pp. 22-23.

13   See, S.K. Bhuyan, *Kamrupar Buranji*, Gauhati, 1930, pp. 64-65; S.K. Bhuyan, *Assam Buranji*, Gauhati, 1945, pp. 82-83; S.K. Dutta, *Assam Buranji*, Gauhati, 1938, pp. 21-22.

14   On behalf of the Ahom, the signatories were the Bura Gohain, Bargohain, Barpatra Gohain, and Phukan, see S.K. Bhuyan, *Atan Buragohain and His Times*, Gauhati, 1957, p. 30.

15   Supungmung established and supervised smithies at his capital for forging weapons, manufacturing gunpowder, and constructing war sloops. He organized a naval fleet and appointed Lachit Bar-Phukan

as the new general. Furthermore, he established friendly alliances with the Koch, Dimasa, and Jaintia rulers, see U.N. Gohain, *Assam Under the Ahoms*, Gauhati, 1942, p. 31.

16 See, S.K. Dutta, *Assam Buranji*, Gauhati, 1938, p. 31; S.K. Bhuyan, *Assam Buranji*, Gauhati, 1945, pp. 99-103.

17 See, S.K. Dutta, *Assam Buranji*, Gauhati, 1938, pp. 31-32; S.K. Bhuyan, *Assam Buranji*, Gauhati, 1945, pp. 103-104; G.C. Barua, *Ahom Buranji*, Gauhati, 1930, pp. 218-221.

18 For a detailed description of Shunyeupha's reign, see G.C. Barua, *Ahom Buranji*, Gauhati, 1930, pp. 292-335; also refer to, S.K. Bhuyan, *Tungkhungia Buranji*, Gauhati, 1933, pp. 61-89.

19 *Mo'tong-deng* ('*mo*' = cooking pot + '*tong-deng*' = copper) means copper cooking pot, see Phukan *et al. Chao-Lung Siu-Ka-Pha*, Guwahati, 1998, p. 21; also refer to G.C. Barua, *Ahom Buranji*, Gauhati, 1930, p. 44.

20 See, G.C. Barua, *Ahom Buranji*, Gauhati, 1930, p. 356; also refer to, S.K. Bhuyan, *Tungkhungia Buranji*, Gauhati, 1933, p. 135.

21 See, G.C. Barua, *Ahom Buranji*, Gauhati, 1930, p.25; also refer to, S.K. Bhuyan, *Satsari Assam Buranji*, Gauhati, 1960, p. 3.

22 *Hilloi-Charanao* was an Ahom war boat laden with various types of artillery, see K. Gogoi, *Ahom Warfare Evolution, Nature, and Strategy* (Ph.D. Thesis), Gauhati, 2017, p. 61.

23 Apart from the mentioned war boats, the Ahom also used other types of boats for transporting goods and people. These were *Charanao, Magarinao, Tulunganao, Panchoi, Kapikal, Haikali, Shihu, Japnao,* and *Chilapati,* see H.K. Barpujari, *The Comprehensive History of Assam* (Vol. 3), Guwahati, 1994, p. 69.

24 The term Dimasa means children of the big river ('*di*' = water + '*ma*' = big + '*sa*' = children), and the river is identified with Dhansiri, which in the Dimasa language is called *Dima*, see A. Tripathi, *Cultural Heritage of Northeast India Recent Perspective*, Delhi, 2019, pp. 171-186.

25 For list of Dimasa monarchs see, S.K. Bhuyan, *Deodhai Assam Buranji*, Gauhati, 1932, p. 133; also refer to S.K. Bhuyan, *Kachari Buranji*, Gauhati, 1936, p. 127.

26   *Chao-Tang* or *Kataki* (similar to *rajdoot*) were court messengers, royal ambassadors or envoys of the Ahom kingdom. They were either sent within the state or to the distant foreign kingdom. Their occupation revolved around delivering messages to and from other countries, carrying on foreign relations during war and peace, and upholding monarchs' honor abroad. The *Katakis* was designated in a hierarchy *Bor* (senior), *Maju* (intermediate), and *Saru* (junior) see, H.K. Barpujari, *The Comprehensive History of Assam*, Vol. 3, Guwahati, 1994, pp. 26-27.

27   Hills in the northern bank of the Brahmaputra River was and still is abode of many ethnic groups, *viz.*, Abor, Dafla, Aka, and Miri, who often raided the villages in the plain. The Ahom devised *Posa* (collection or subscription) system to prevent such raids. According to the *Posa* system, chiefs were allowed to levy and collect an annual tax from every household in a particular village, instead of raiding them. For further explanation, see P. Goswami, *The History of Assam: From Yandabo to Partition 1826-1947*, New Delhi, 2012, pp. 150-151.

28   See, S.K. Dutta, *Assam Buranji*, Gauhati, 1938, pp. 9-10; G.C. Barua, *Ahom Buranji*, Gauhati, 1930, pp. 153-154.

29   See, S.K. Bhuyan, *Tungkhungia Buranji*, Gauhati, 1933, pp. 24-25; G.C. Barua, *Ahom Buranji*, Gauhati, 1930, p. 267.

30   The total number of artilleries collected by the Ahom during the Ahom-Chutiya war varies in chronicles. For instance, according to the *Deodhai Assam Buranji* (Bhuyan 1932) and the *Assam Buranji* (Bhuyan 1945) the Ahom collected one thousand artilleries from the Chutiya while the *Satsari Assam Buranji* (Bhuyan 1960) refer to only seventy-nine artilleries.

31   See, V. Ball, *Travels in India by Jean Baptiste Tavernier*, Vol. 2, London, 1889, p. 277.

32   There is ambiguity among scholars regarding the commander of these divisions. For example, Gogoi's (2017) account contradicts Barpujari's (1994) account. According to Gogoi (2017), the *Bajua-Hilloidhari-Konwar* was under the command of *Naoboicha Phukan* and not *Hilloidhari Phukan*. Similarly, *Bhitarual-Hilloidhari-Konwar* was under the command of *Bhitarual Phukan* and not *Hilloidhari Barua*.

33 See, G.C. Barua, *Ahom Buranji*, Gauhati, 1930, p. 18; K.T. Phukan, *Assam Buranji*, Gauhati, 1844, p. 3.

34 During the Ahom rule, entire male population within the age group of fifteen and fifty were organized and divided into units of *Paik*, who offered their specific services to the state. This system was known as the *Khel* (guild) system. For further discussion on *Khel* system see, H.K. Barpujari, *The Comprehensive History of Assam*, Vol. 3, Guwahati, 1994, pp. 36-42.

35 The *Satsari Assam Buranji* (Bhuyan 1960) provides a detail of the families who migrated to the Ahom capital. These were families of *Bamun* (brahmana), *Ganak* (astrologer), and also other families of artisan and craftsmen, *viz.*, *Sonari* (goldsmith), blacksmith, *Teli* (oil-extractor), *Mali* (gardener), *Dhoba* (washermen), and *Tati* (weaver).

36 Apart from pig iron, other trading articles from the Khasi-Jaintia Hills include wax, ivory, cotton, betel leaf, and cloth, see, W. Robinson, *A Descriptive Account of Assam*, Gauhati, 1841, p. 408; also refer to R.B. Pemberton, *Report on the Eastern Frontier of British India*, Calcutta, 1835, p. 215.

37 See, V. Ball, *Travels in India by Jean Baptiste Tavernier*, Vol. 2, London, 1889, pp. 277-279.

Color Illustration of Weapons

Color Illustration of Jathi (1-10) (*source*: author)

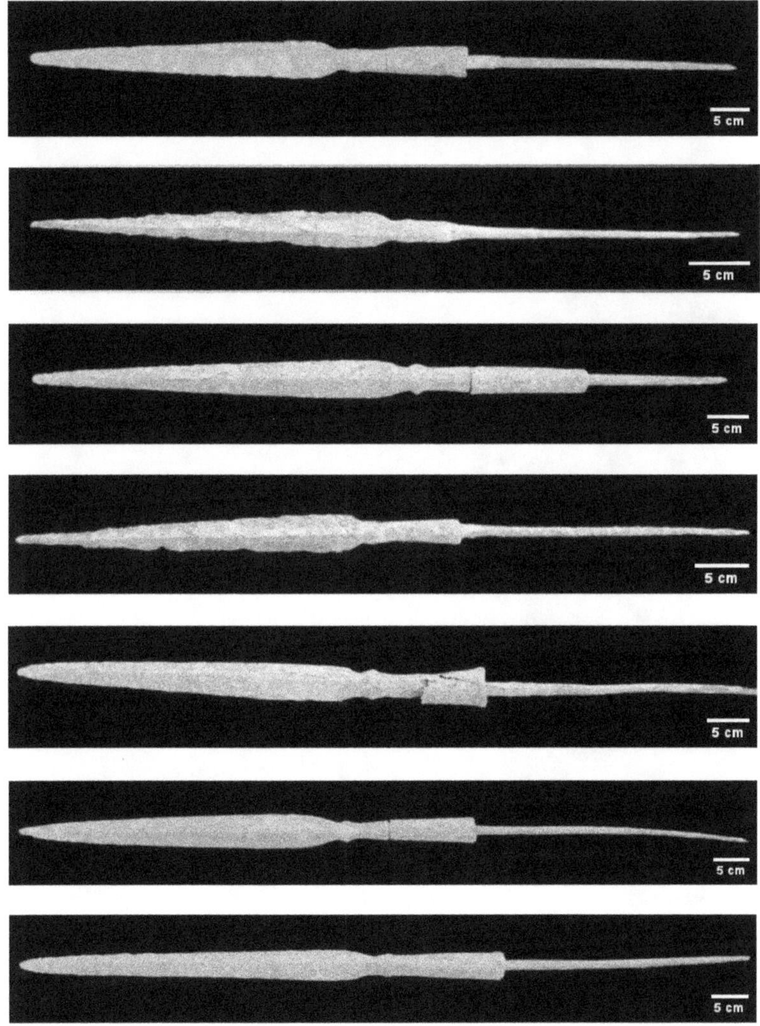

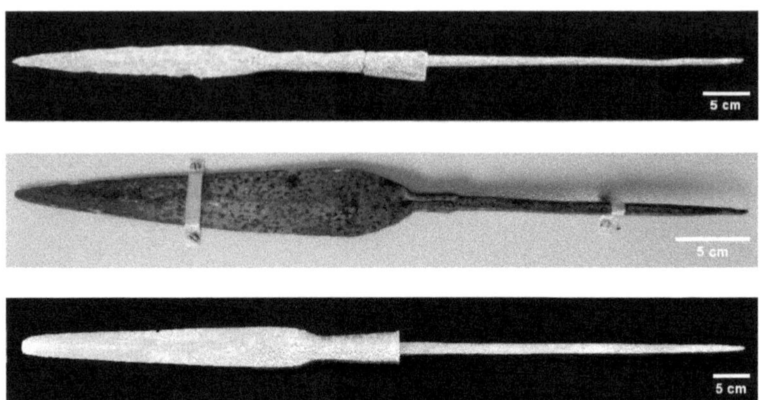

Color Illustration of Barsha (1-4) (*source*: author)

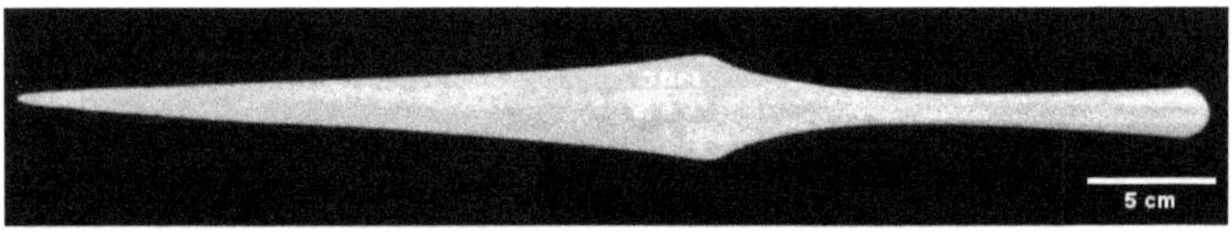

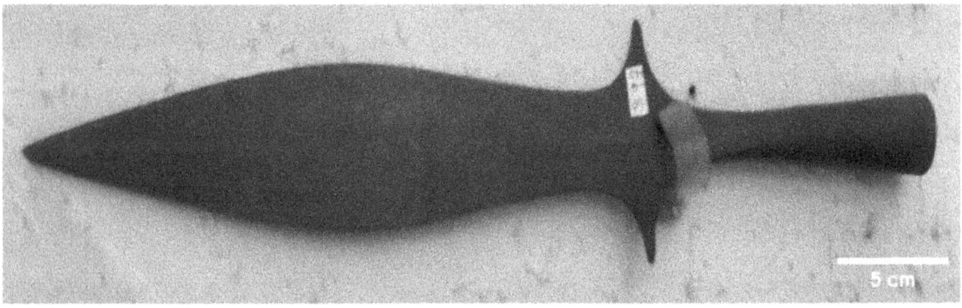

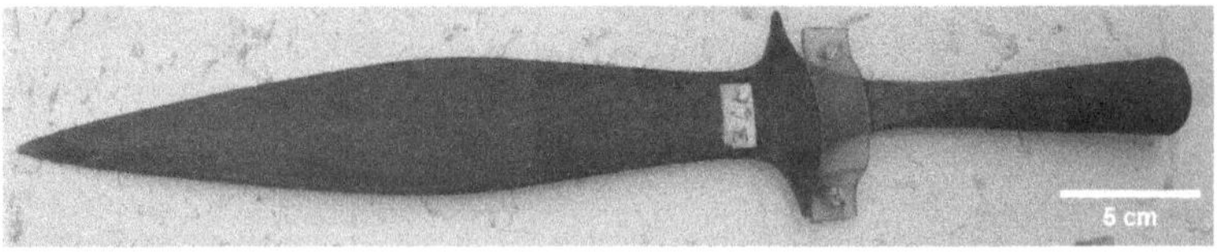

Color Illustration of Khapor 1 (*source*: author)

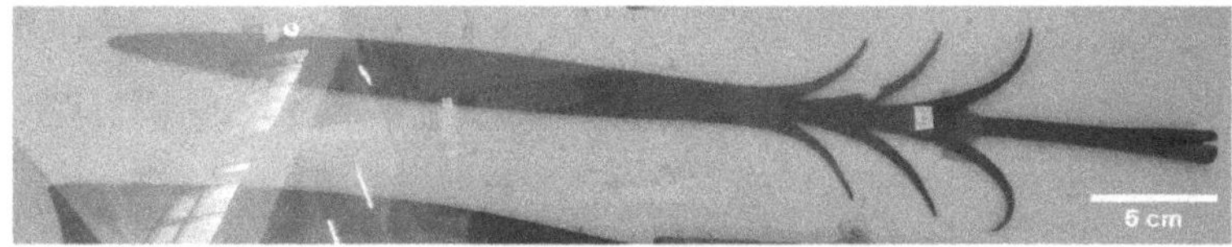

Color Illustration of Hengdang (1-2) (*source*: author)

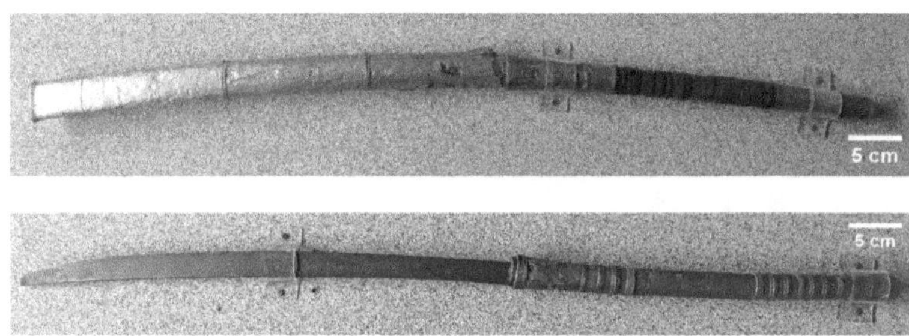

Color Illustration of Torowal (1-6) (*source*: author)

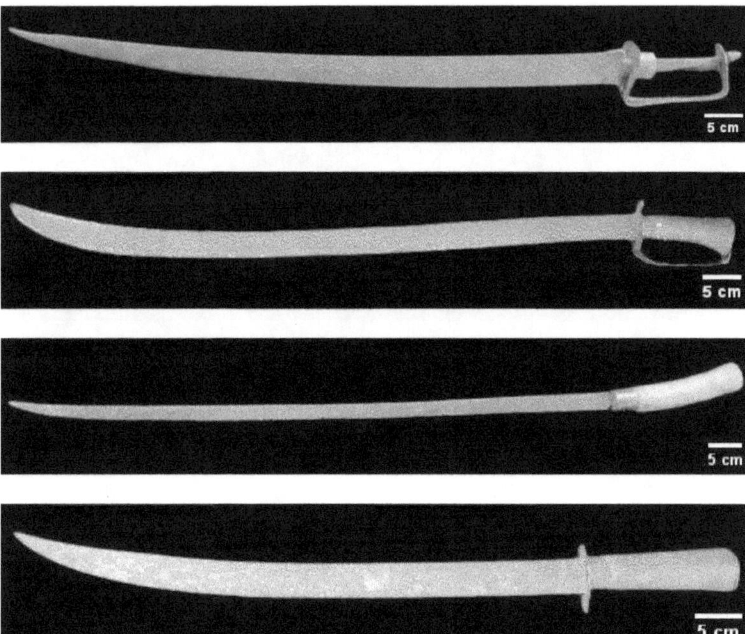

Color Illustration of Nakoi-da (1-8) (*source*: author)

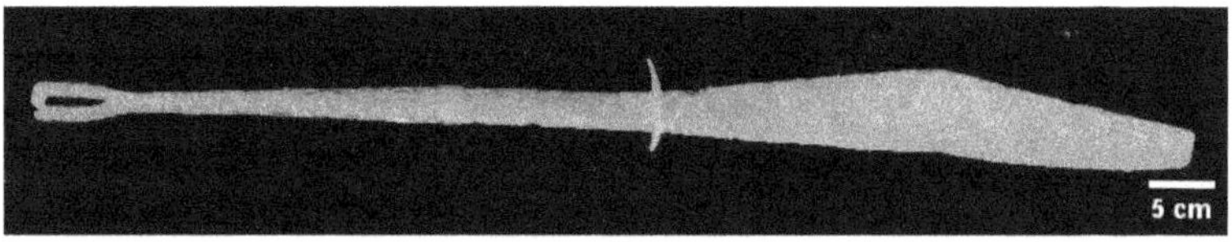

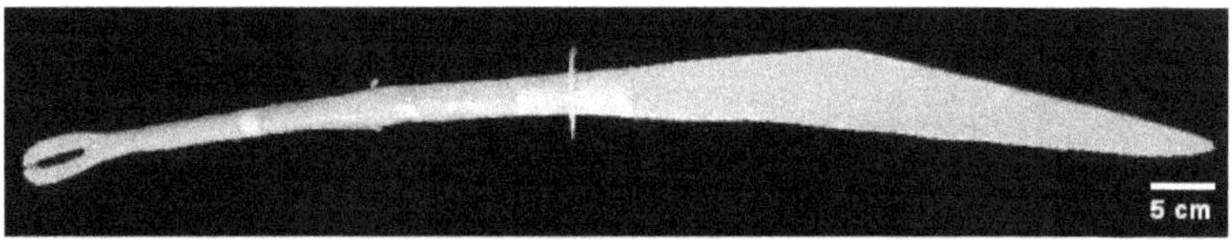

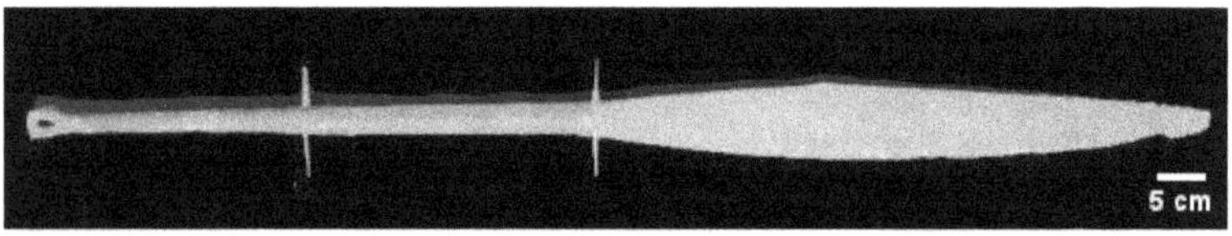

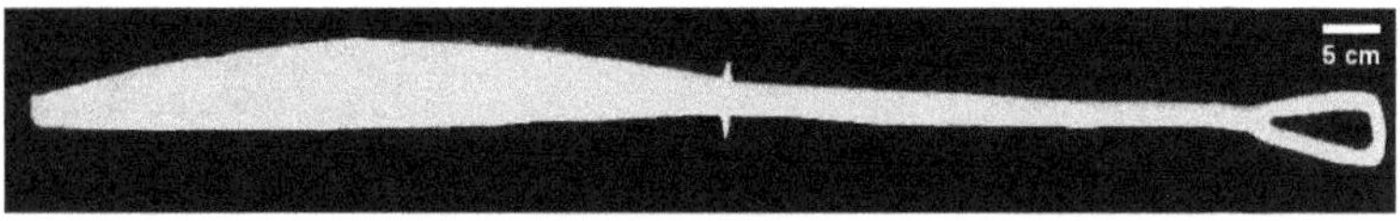

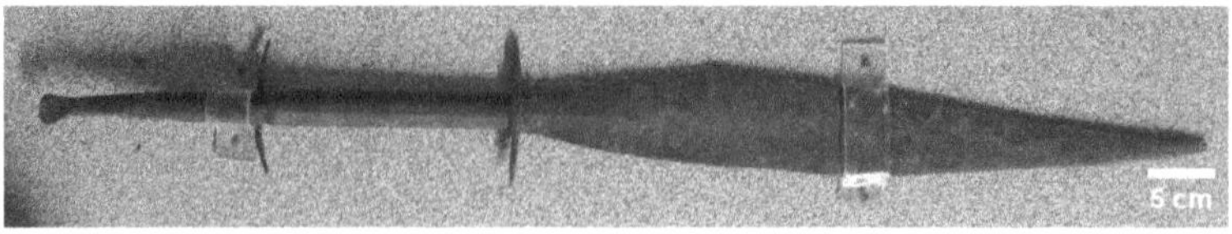

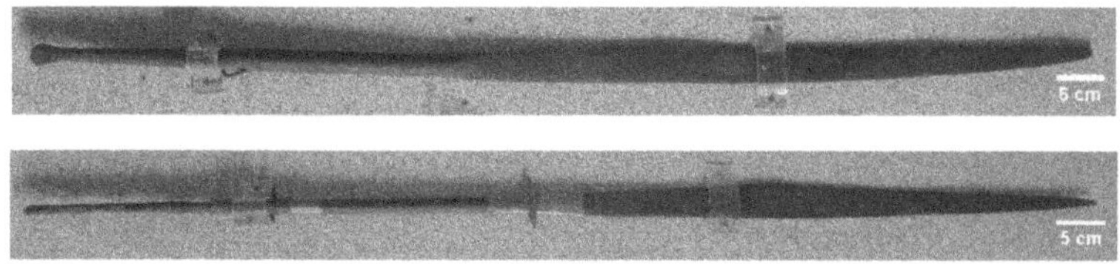

Color Illustration of Shikara-da 1 (*source*: author)

Color Illustration of Heavy Artillery or Bortop at Talatalghar, Sivasagar (*source*: author)

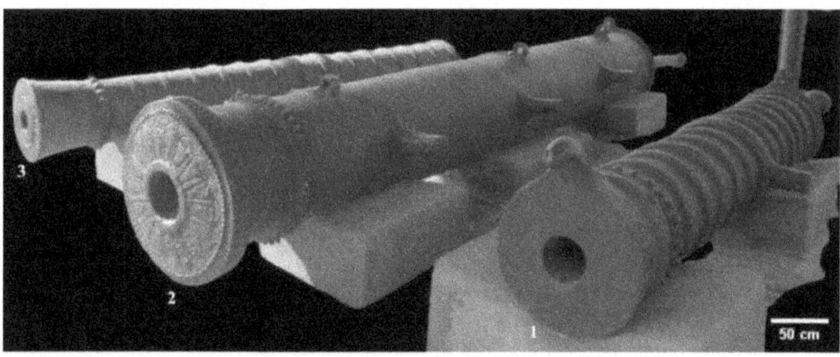

Color Illustration of Heavy Artillery at District Museum, Jorhat (*source*: author)

Color Illustration of Heavy Artillery at District Museum, Dibrugarh (*source*: author)

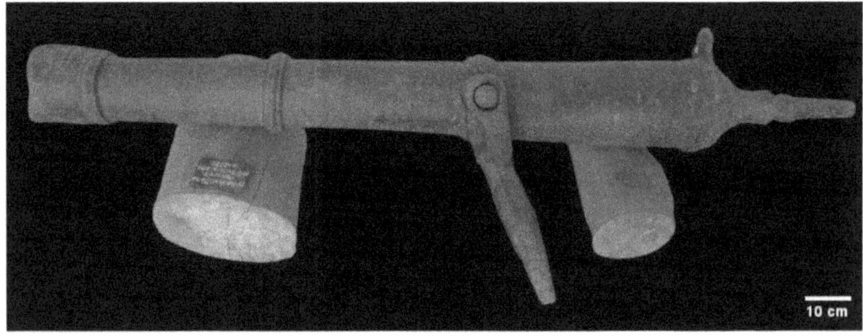

Color Illustration of Heavy Artillery at District Museum, Tezpur (*source*: author)

Color Illustration of Heavy Artillery at Assam State Museum, Guwahati (17-23) (*source*: author)

Color Illustration of Light Artillery or Hilloi at Assam State Museum, Guwahati (1-2) (*source*: author)

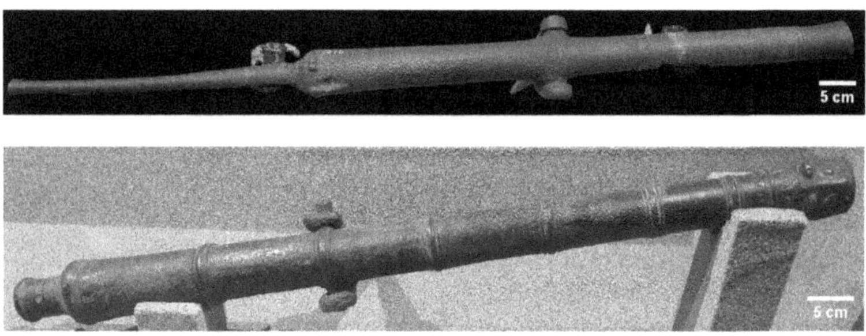

Color Illustration of Light Artillery at District Museum, Jorhat (3-4) (*source*: author)

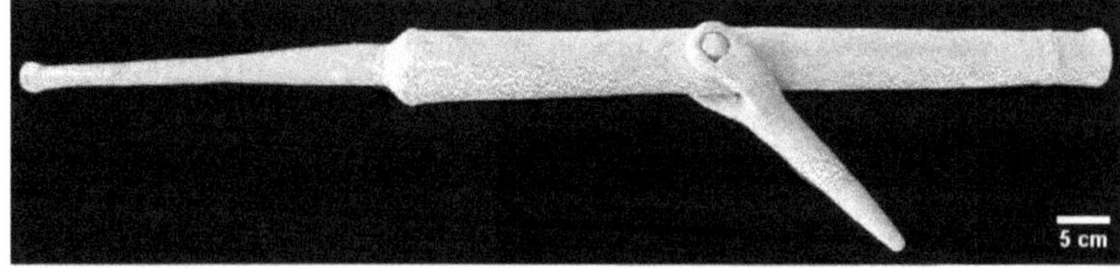

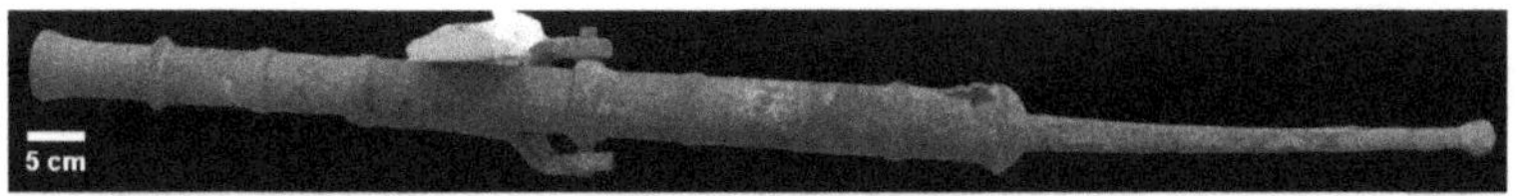

Color Illustration of Light Artillery at District Museum, Dibrugarh (5-6) (*source*: author)

Color Illustration of Light Artillery at Ahom Tai Museum, Sivasagar (7-10) (*source*: author)

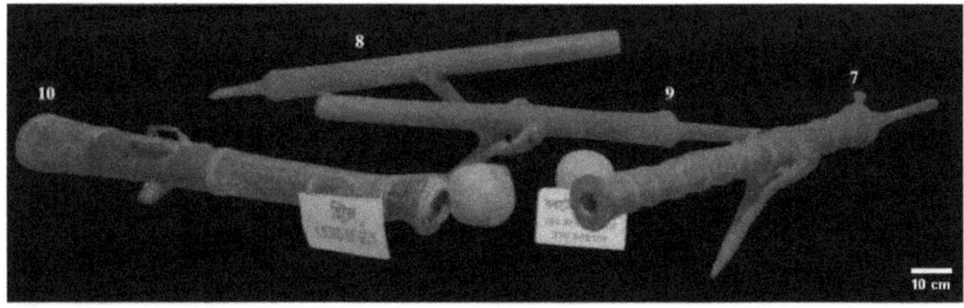

Color Illustration of Cannon Ball at District Museum, Dibrugarh (left), Asssam State Museum (right), and District Museum, Jorhat (below) (*source*: author)

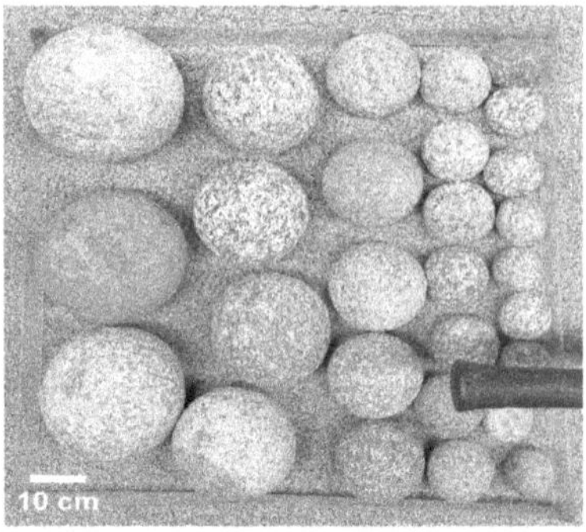

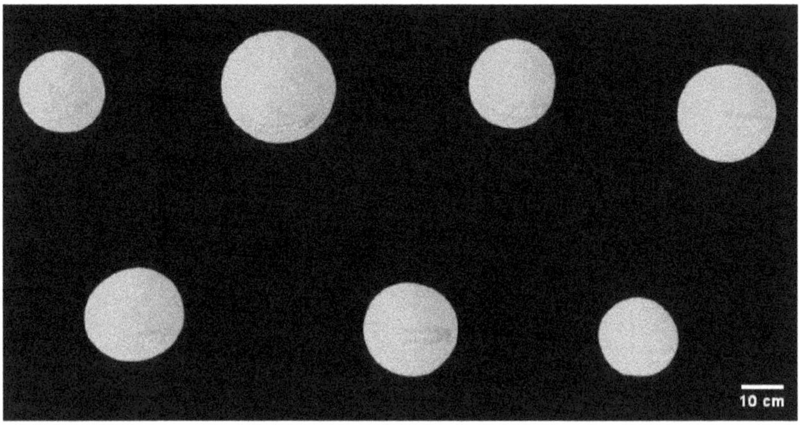

Color Illustration of Shield at District Museum, Dibrugarh (left), Assam State Museum, Guwahati (center), and Ahom Tai Museum, Sivasagar (right) (*source*: author)

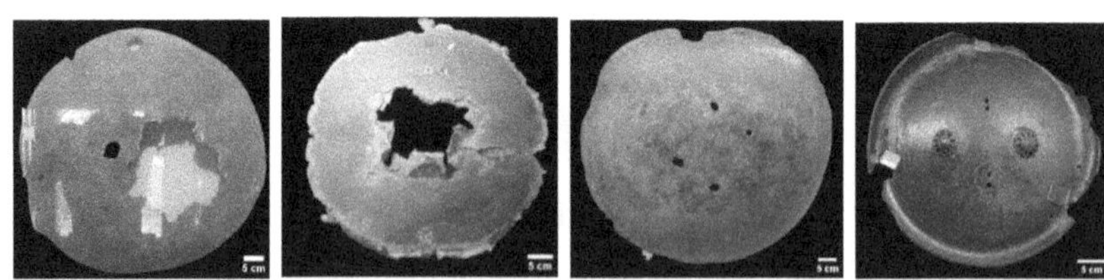

Appendix 1

<table>
<tr><td colspan="2" align="center">Pro Forma for Recording Edged Weapon</td></tr>
<tr><td colspan="2">Measurement (length in centimetre and weight in kilogram)</td></tr>
<tr><td>1.   Weapon name</td><td></td></tr>
<tr><td>2.   Location</td><td></td></tr>
<tr><td>3.   Accession number</td><td></td></tr>
<tr><td>4.   Period</td><td></td></tr>
<tr><td>5.   Full length</td><td></td></tr>
<tr><td>6.   Weight</td><td></td></tr>
<tr><td>7.   Point of balance</td><td></td></tr>
</table>

Blade measurement (all in centimetre)

1. Blade length [ ]   2. Cross-section [ ]

3. Ricasso length [ ]   4. Fuller (if any) [ ]

5. Blade point [ ]   6. Point of percussion (from the tip) [ ]

7. Base width [ ]   8. Base thickness [ ]

2/3 width [ ]   2/3 thickness [ ]

1/3 width [ ]   1/3 thickness [ ]

Condition/damage/decoration

[ ]

Handle measurement (all in centimetre)

1. Handle length [ ]   2. Cross-section [ ]

3. Ferrule length (if any) [ ]   4. Langet length (if any) [ ]

5. Tang length (if visible) [ ]   6. Cross-guard length (if any) [ ]

7. Pommel radius (if any) [ ]

Notes

[ ]

Appendix 2

Pro Forma for Recording Cannon and Hand Cannon

Measurement (length in centimetre and weight in kilogram)

1. Weapon name

2. Location

3. Accession number

4. Period

5. Full length

6. Weight

Condition/damage/decoration/inscription

All measurement in centimetre

7. Barrel length

8. Trunnion length

9. Trunnion diameter

10. Vent/Touch Hole diameter

11. External diameter of Muzzle

12. Bore diameter

13. Knob length

14.	Circumference of Knob	
15.	External diameter of Breech	
16.	Distance between Vent and Breech base	
17.	Trunnion to Muzzle length	
18.	Trunnion to Breech base length	

Notes

Appendix 3

<table>
<tr><td colspan="3" align="center">***Pro Forma* for Recording Shield**</td></tr>
<tr><td colspan="3">**Measurement (length in centimetre and weight in kilogram)**</td></tr>
<tr><td>1.</td><td>Weapon name</td><td></td></tr>
<tr><td>2.</td><td>Location</td><td></td></tr>
<tr><td>3.</td><td>Accession number</td><td></td></tr>
<tr><td>4.</td><td>Period</td><td></td></tr>
<tr><td>5.</td><td>Weight</td><td></td></tr>
<tr><td>6.</td><td>Shape</td><td></td></tr>
<tr><td>7.</td><td>Diameter</td><td></td></tr>
<tr><td colspan="3">Condition/damage/decoration</td></tr>
<tr><td colspan="3">

</td></tr>
<tr><td colspan="3">Notes

</td></tr>
</table>

Glossary

Angar	Charcoal
Bachari	Ahom war boat
Bar-dhenu	A type of bow used by the Bhuyans that was later acquired and used by the Ahom
Barsha	Leaf-shaped spear
Biagom	A type of Ahom heavy artillery
Bortop	Ahom heavy artillery, also called *Klang-lung*
Buranji	Ahom chronicles (*'bu'*= ignorant + *'ran'* = person + *'ji'* = store)
Chak-lang	Ahom marriage
Chandraban	A type of Ahom rocket
Chaopha	Ahom monarch
Chao-Tang	Kataki (royal ambassador)
Che-Din-Chi-Pen	Present-day Dimapur, the then capital of the Dimasa kingdom
Chehung	Garhgaon

Che-Tam-Doi	Charaideo
Choi	Tribute
Chutiya-dhenu	A type of bow used by the Chutiya that was later acquired and used by the Ahom
Da	Chopper
Dhal	Circular shield made of animal hide
Dhenu	Bow
Doi-Kao-Rong	Identified with the Patkai Hills (*'doi'* = mountain + *'kao'* = nine + *'rong'* = unite or meet)
Duta	Javelin
Gati	Jacket
Ghora-Barua	Officer in charge of the royal stable
Ghorasal	Royal stable
Gulli	Cannon Ball
Habung	The area between Dihing and Lohit River
Hadora	An open-hearth furnace
Hat	Market
Hati-Barbora	Officer-in-charge of the royal elephants
Hatina	Bellow

Hatisal	A place where trained elephants were kept
Haturi	Hammer
Hengdang	A single-edged curved sword used by the Ahom
Hengdang-dhara	Wielder of a Hengdang
Hilloi	Ahom light artillery, also called *Klang-noi*
Hilloi-Charanao	Ahom war boat
Hilloidari	Guild, who used a firearm
Jang-Ti-Ma	Doyang River
Jathi	Flat-spear
Jayta kingdom	Jaintia kingdom
Kamar	Blacksmith
Kamateswar	Kamata monarch
Kar	Arrow
Khamjang	A river that originates from Nongyang Lake and meets at the Chindwin River
Khamrap	Identified with Kamrup, present-day Guwahati
Khan-Rang-You	Barahi ethnic group
Khapor	Multi-barbed spear

Khedashikar	One of the two methods to capture wild elephant
Khel	Guild
Kheldar	Officer in charge of a guild
Konwar	Ahom prince
Konwar-Hilloidari	The guild comprising Ahom princes who wielded a firearm
Kring-lang or Got	The lowest unit in the paik system comprising three to four members
Kush	Ahom war boat
Kusha	Ahom war boat
Lik	Iron
Lik-Khang	Iron ladder
Losalia	Also known as Tiruwal, it was a guild engaged with the mining and smelting of iron ore in the Ahom kingdom.
Magalu	Manipur
Manah	Manas River
Mantara	Burma (present-day Republic of the Union of Myanmar)
Maranki	Marangi
Marnao	Ahom war boat

Mast	Elephant heat
Maut	Elephant trainer
Melashikar	Method to capture a wild elephant
Methon	Wild cow
Mithaholong	A type of Ahom heavy artillery that was acquired from the Chutiya kingdom
Mo'tong-deng	Copper-made cooking pots
Mong	Province
Mong-Dun-Sun-Kham	Ahom kingdom (*'mong'* = province + *'dun'* = full + *'sun'* = garden + *'kham'* = gold)
Mongmao	Tai Province in southwestern China
Nakoi-da	A type of chopper used by the Dimasa
Nam-Deng	Identified with Namdang River (*'nam'* = water + *'deng'* = red)
Nam-Jin	Buri Dihing River (*'nam'* = water + *'jin'* = cold)
Nam-Sao	Dikhow River (*'nam'* = water + *'sao'* = clear)
Nam-Ti-Lao	Brahmaputra River
Nam-Ti-Ma	Dhansiri River
Naoboicha	Ahom navy

Naora	Water pot used for quenching
Naosal	Dockyard
Nara-Hilloidari	The guild comprised of the Nara ethnic group who wielded a firearm.
Niyari	Anvil
Nongyang Lake	Also known as the "Lake of No Return," it is on the India-Myanmar border
Ojha	Head smelter
Paik	They were the able male citizens who provided compulsory civil and military service to the Ahom monarchy.
Palee	Smelter's assistant
Phang kingdom	Kamata kingdom
Phar	Long shield made of bamboo or cane
Phrang-Mong-Lung	Burha Gohain
Phu-Kan	Phukan
Phu-Kan-Lung	Bar Phukan
Phu-Kao	Moran ethnic group
Phu-Ke-Lung	Bar Barua
Phu-Kin-Mong	Rajkhowa
Ramchangi	A type of Ahom light artillery
Ru-Pak	Saikia

Ru-Ring	Hazarika
Ru-Sao	Bora
Sarfil	A herb that was applied on male elephants to bring heat within twenty-four hour
Seng-Lung	Barpatra Gohain
Shikara-da	Also known as *Miri-da*, it was a chopper used by the Miri ethnic group
Subahdar	Mughal Governor
Takaya	Helmet
Tangan horse	Horses from Bhutan
Thao-Mong-Lung	Bar Gohain
Thao-Mong-Maranki	Marangi Khowa Gohain
Thao-Mong-Tiora	Sadiya Khowa Gohain
Tikarai	Dikrai River
Timisa	Dimasa ethnic group
Tiora	Chutiya ethnic group
Tipam	The present-day area around Jeypore in Dibrugarh district, Assam ('*ti*' = place + '*pam*' = river bank)
Tiru Hill	It is located in the present-day Mon district in Nagaland

Torowal	Sword
Xel	Barbed spear
Xul	Rod spear
Zambur	A type of Mughal light artillery

Bibliography

Acharyya, N.N. (1966) *The History of Medieval Assam* (2003, reprint). New Delhi: Omsons Publications.

Allen, W.J. (1858) *Report on the Administration of the Cossyas and Jynteah Hill Territory*. Calcutta: John Gray Bengal Hurkaru Press.

Baishya, D. (2009) *Traditional Science and Material Culture of Early Assam*. Guwahati: E.H.B. Publisher.

Ball, V. (trans.). (1889) *Travels in India by Jean Baptiste Tavernier* (Vol. 2). London: Macmillan and Co.

Barpujari, H.K. (ed.). (1992) *The Comprehensive History of Assam* (2010, 4th ed., Vol. 2). Guwahati: Publication Board Assam.

Barpujari, H.K. (ed.). (1994) *The Comprehensive History of Assam* (2007, 3rd ed., Vol. 3). Guwahati: Publication Board Assam.

Barua, K.L. (1933) *Early History of Kamarupa* (1988, 3rd. ed.). Gauhati: Lawyers Book Stall.

Barua, R.S.G. (trans.). (1930) *Ahom Buranji from the Earliest Time to the End of Ahom Rule* (2016, reprint). Gauhati: Spectrum Publication.

Baruah, S.L. (1985) *A Comprehensive History of Assam* (2007, ed.). New Delhi: Munshiram Manoharlal Publishers Pvt. Ltd.

Bhattacharya, S.N. (1929) *A History of Mughal North-East Frontier Policy* (1998, reprint). Gauhati: Spectrum Publications.

Bhuyan, S.K. (1930) *Kamrupar Buranji* (2017, 5th ed.). Gauhati: Department of Historical and Antiquarian Studies (DHAS).

Bhuyan, S.K. (1957) *Atan Buragohain and His Times* (1992, 2nd ed.). Gauhati: Lawyer's Book Stall.

Bhuyan, S.K. (ed. and trans.). (1933) *Tungkhungia Buranji* (2012, 4th ed.). Gauhati: DHAS.

Bhuyan, S.K. (ed.). (1930) *Assam Buranji by the Late Harakanta Barua Sadar-Amin*. Gauhati: DHAS.

Bhuyan, S.K. (ed.). (1932) *Deodhai Assam Buranji* (2001, 4th ed.). Gauhati: DHAS.

Bhuyan, S.K. (ed.). (1936) *Kachari Buranji* (2010, 4th ed.). Gauhati: DHAS.

Bhuyan, S.K. (ed.). (1937) *Jayantia Buranji* (2012, 3rd ed.). Gauhati: DHAS.

Bhuyan, S.K. (ed.). (1945) *Assam Buranji* (2010, 4th ed.). Gauhati: DHAS.

Bhuyan, S.K. (ed.). (1960) *Satsari Assam Buranji*. Gauhati: Gauhati University.

Blochmann, H. (1872) Koch Bihar, Koch Hajo, and A'sam, in the 16th and 17th centuries, according to the Akbarnamah, the Padishahnamah, and the Fathiyah i 'Ibriyah. *Journal of the Asiatic Society of Bengal, 41*, 49–101.

Borah, M.I. (trans.). (1936) *Baharistan-i-Ghaybi* (1992, 2nd ed., Vol. 2). Gauhati: DHAS.

Borboruah, H. (1981) *Ahomar Din* (1997, 2nd ed.). Gauhati: Publication Board Assam.

Buragohain, N. (2022) *Ahom Jugar Hiloi Bartop*. Guwahati: J. S. Publication.

Choudhury, J.N. (1978) *The Khasi Canvas*. Calcutta: Bavana Printing Works Private Ltd.

Cracroft, W. (1832) Smelting of Iron in the Kasya Hills. *Journal of the Asiatic Society of Bengal, 1*, 150–151.

Devi, L. (1968) *Ahom Tribal Relations A Political Study* (1992, 2nd ed.). Gauhati: Lawyer's Book Stall.

Dutta, S.K. (1938) *Assam Buranji 1648-1681* (1991, 2nd ed.). Gauhati: DHAS.

Gait, E. (1905) *A History of Assam* (2012, reprint). Gauhati: E.B.H. Publishers.

Gogoi, K. (2017) *Ahom Warfare Evolution, Nature, and Strategy* (Ph.D. Thesis). Gauhati University.

Gogoi, N.K. (2006) *Continuity and Change Among the Ahoms*. New Delhi: Concept Publishing Company.

Gogoi, P. (2006) War Weapons in Medieval Assam. In S. Dutta and B. Tripathy (eds.), *Martial Traditions of North-East India*. New Delhi: Concept Publishing Company.

Gohain, B.K. (1999) *Origin of the Tai and Chao Lung Hsukapha*. New Delhi: Omsons Publications.

Gohain, U.N. (1942) *Assam Under the Ahoms* (1999, reprint). Gauhati: Spectrum Publications.

Goodrich, L.C., and Chia-sheng, F. (1946) The Early Development of Firearms in China. *Isis, 36*(2), 114-123.

Goswami, H. (ed.). (1922) *Purani Assam Buranji* (1977, 2nd ed.). Gauhati: Lawyer's Book Stall.

Goswami, P. (2012) *The History of Assam from Yandobo to Partition 1826-1947*. New Delhi: Orient Black Swan.

Hamilton, F. (1940) *An Account of Assam* (1987, 3rd ed., S.K. Bhuyan, ed.). Gauhati: DHAS.

Hannay, S.F. (1856) Iron Ore Statistics and Economic Geology of Upper Assam. *Journal of the Asiatic Society of Bengal, 25*, 330–344.

Hrisoulas, J. (1987) *The Complete Bladesmith Forging Your Way to Perfection*. Colorado: Paladin Press.

Hunter, W.W. (1879) *A Statistical Account of Assam* (Vol. 2). London: Trubner and Co.

Kalita, B. (1988) *Military Activities in Medieval Assam* (2012, 2nd ed.). Gauhati: DHAS.

Khan, I.A. (1994) The Role of the Mongols in the Introduction of Gunpowder and Firearms in India. *Proceedings of the Indian History Congress, 55*, 194-200.

Khan, S.U. (1947) *Maasir-i-Alamgiri* (J. Sarkar, trans.). Calcutta: Royal Asiatic Society of Bengal.

Lahiri, R.M. (1954) *The Annexation of Assam* (2003, reprint). Calcutta: Firma KLM Private Limited.

Laichen, S. (2003) Military Technology Transfers from Ming China and the Emergence of Northern Mainland Southeast Asia. *Journal of Southeast Asian Studies, 34*(3), 495-517.

Leach, E.R. (1954) *Political Systems of Highland Burma A Study of Kachin Social Structure* (1970, reprint). London: The Athlone Press.

Ling, W. (1947) On the Invention and Use of Gunpowder and Firearms in China. *Isis, 37*(3/4), 160-178.

Lish, A.B. (1838) Brief Account of the Khasees. *The Calcutta Christian Observer, 7*, 129–143.

M'Cosh, J. (1837) *Topography of Assam.* Calcutta: Bengal Military Orphan Press.

Mills, A.J.M. (1853) *Reports on the Khasi and Jaintia Hills.* Shillong: Authority.

Nath, R.M. (1948) *The Background of the Assamese Culture* (1978, 2nd ed.). Gauhati: Dutta Baruah and Co.

Nath, S. (2023) Bolikota-da: Types and Description. *Aalekh, 2*(4), 53-57.

Nath, S. (2024) Ahom-Miri Relation and the Exchange of Shikara-da. *Aalekh, 3*(5), 66-69.

Oldham, T. (1859) *Memoirs of the Geological Survey of India* (Vol. 1). Calcutta: Government of India.

Pemberton, R.B. (1835) *Report on the Eastern Frontier of British India*. Calcutta: Government of India.

Phukan, H.D. (1962) *Assam Buranji* (J.M. Bhattacharjee, ed.). Gauhati: Mokshada Publication.

Phukan, J.N. (1973) *The Economic History of Assam Under the Ahoms* (Ph.D. Thesis). Gauhati University.

Phukan, J.N., Buragohain, R., and Buragohain, Y.H. (trans.). (1998) *Chao-Lung Siu-Ka-Pha* (Vol. 1). Guwahati: The Celebration Committee 770th anniversary of Chao-Lung Siu-Ka-Pha.

Phukan, K.N.T. (1844) *Assam Buranji* (2015, 3rd ed.). Gauhati: DHAS.

Purkayastha, S. (2007) Iron Industry in the Brahmaputra Valley: Losalias and the Kamars (Late Medieval to mid Colonial Period). *The Indian Historical Review, 34*(1), 152–166.

Robinson, W. (1841) *A Descriptive Account of Assam* (reprint). Delhi: Sanskaran Prakashak.

Salim, G.H. (1902) *Riyaz-us-Salatin* (M.A. Salam, trans.). Calcutta: Asiatic Society.

Sarkar, J. N. (1915). Assam and the Ahoms in 1660 A.D. *Journal of the Bihar and Orissa Research Society, 1*, 179–195.

Sarkar, J.N. (1916) *History of Aurangzeb* (1928, 3rd ed., Vol. 3). Calcutta: Sarkar and Sons.

Sarkar, J.N. (1951) *The Life of Mir Jumla: The General of Aurangzeb*. Calcutta: Thacker, Spink and Co.

Sarma, B. (1950) *Maniram Dewan*. Gauhati (1994, 3rd ed). Gauhati: Manuh Prakashan.

Sharma, C.K. (1996) Socio-Economic Structure and Peasant Revolt the Case of Moamoria Upsurge in the Eighteenth Century Assam. *Indian Anthropologist, 26*(2), 33-52.

Tripathi, A and Nath, S. (2024) Ahom Hengdang: Types and Description. *Aalekh, 3*(5), 14-20.

Tripathi, A. and Langthasa, S. (2019) Dimasa Monuments: Types and Architecture. In A. Tripathi (ed.), *Cultural Heritage of Northeast India Recent Perspective*. Delhi: Sharada Publishing House.

Wade, J.P. (1800) *An Account of Assam* (B. Sarma, ed.). North Lakhimpur: R. Sarma Madhupur Tea Estate.

www.ingramcontent.com/pod-product-compliance
Lightning Source LLC
Chambersburg PA
CBHW041328120726

48005CB00014B/2165